Aurelius Graf von Staufen

# THE GLOBAL INVESTOR

How to protect your family,

your capital and yourself!

Bibliografische Information der Deutschen Nationalbibliothek:
Die Deutsche Nationalbibliothek verzeichnet diese Publikation in der
Deutschen Nationalbibliografie; detaillierte bibliografische Daten sind im
Internet über http://dnb.dnb.de abrufbar.

© 2022 Aurelius Graf von Staufen

Herstellung und Verlag: BoD – Books on Demand, Norderstedt

ISBN: 978-3-7543-6013-2

# Contents

PROLOGUE ............................................................................. 9

INTRODUCTION ................................................................... 11

PT- PERMANENT TRAVELER .............................................. 13

TAX HAVEN .......................................................................... 23

TOTAL ANONYMITY ............................................................ 93

GOLD AS AN INVESTMENT ............................................... 108

CRYPTOCURRENCIES ......................................................... 161

FOREIGN INVESTMENTS ................................................... 179

THE WORLD MONEY SCAM .............................................. 186

SECOND PASSPORT- WHY DO I NEED A SECOND PASSPORT OR CITIZENSHIP? ............................................................................................. 193

THE DIPLOMATIC PASSPORT ........................................... 215

SUMMARY .......................................................................... 223

EPILOGUE ........................................................................... 225

APPENDIX: Vienna Convention on Consular Relations Done at Vienna on 24 April 1963 ......................................................................... 226

APPENDIX: Vienna Convention on Diplomatic Relations Done at Vienna on 18 April 1961 .................................................................... 285

I

# PROLOGUE

**THE GLOBAL INVESTOR** How to protect your family, your capital and yourself! Aurelius Count von Staufen

The extent of the Corona crisis is far from clear, but one thing is absolutely certain: your fundamental and human rights are in danger and well on their way to disappearing permanently. Not only since the revelations of Edward Snowden and Julian Assagne is your privacy more important than ever before; these revelations just confirmed what insiders have known for years.

This book will show you how to protect your privacy, family and assets as best as you can and what you need to consider. You will receive in-depth details, factual accounts, and real-world case studies with corresponding contact information. It doesn`t matter if you are looking for an appropriate offshore jurisdiction for your foreign company or if you have decided on a new citizenship, you will be introduced to the subject with this publication. More and more indebted countries are trying to have their citizens from the middle to the upper class pay heavily or may even abolish the middle class altogether in the near future. The Corona crisis is assisting in this effort. It is also a fact that most countries are just as broke as Argentina. This country has already been insolvent several times in just a few years. However, these facts are only concealed and hidden from the normal citizen and voter. As a result of the Corona crisis, more money is being printed and put into circulation than ever before.

But even these financial packages, which are already being put together on a weekly basis, have to be paid for and financed by someone at some point. Make an educated guess who is going to pay for all that.

Those who no longer want all this should also pack their bags as soon as possible or at least prepare themselves for the coming years! In this book you will find explanations and suggestions for a carefree, tax-free and reasonably anonymous life. Start making the appropriate arrangements today, before it's too late. You will find the right instructions to help you get an immediate start abroad, whether you want or need to go as a millionaire or due to bankruptcy. It will be explained to you step by step how you can make a new start in order to not fall into the typical Becker or Hoeneß trap. You have already taken the first step by buying this book, for which I congratulate you!

# INTRODUCTION

My task here is not to join the ranks of conspiracy theorists in order to analyze the Corona crisis for you or to explain its origins; you can do this best by yourself. I also cannot and do not want to discuss whether the mask obligation makes sense or not, or who earns money from a possible vaccine, or whether the infection figures are right or wrong and on which sources they are based at all.

What I can draw attention to, however, is the fact that with the help of the Corona crisis there are more and more massive restrictions on your human and fundamental rights. Your private life, your business, your freedom of movement and your freedom of expression are being very severely restricted. This is all coupled with an impending vaccination requirement that can be legally imposed on you via the recently passed Emergency Law.

This has been made possible for the legislature in this form only since the Corona crisis and mostly without any opposition from the population. The aim of this book is to show you the last remaining solutions which you can still use in the next one to three years to position yourself accordingly for your family and your capital and to prepare for the coming events. This applies equally to both private individuals and entrepreneurs.

Your life planning must remain in your hands!

Over the course of several chapters, I will describe various strategies and possibilities. At the end of the book, I will summarize everything for you again. Even if you cannot apply all strategies and solutions, even parts of them can help you considerably to survive the coming years and to shape them yourself.

# PT- PERMANENT TRAVELER

## The PT Philosophy

PT usually refers to a permanent traveler or permanent "tax saver".

It can also mean PERMANENT TOURIST/PERMANENT TAX AVOIDER / PRIOR TAXPAYER / PERPETUAL TRAVELER. These or similar expressions are used for this grouping.

Permanent Traveler can thus be both a form of lifestyle and a philosophy.

A PT is usually defined as a group of people who have arranged their lives in such a way that they are not really resident in any country, or at least are not registered in the countries where they regularly reside or do business. Through this way of life of "non-residence," PTs try to avoid their obligations as citizens, such as paying taxes, complying with certain laws, and completing military service.

Most PTs do not live in a particular country for more than 3 months at a time while residing in a country other than the one where they hold citizenship, usually in a tax haven. This version or philosophy of life is especially popular and suitable for wealthy Europeans.

For example, as a citizen of Germany, France or the United Kingdom, you can simply move your residence to Monaco or Campione and you are therefore no longer liable to tax in Germany, since in Germany the tax liability is linked to your place of residence.

The German 183-day rule and a possible departure taxation must also be taken into account here.

This is much more difficult for an American citizen, because even if he emigrates from the USA forever and moves his residence to a tax haven, he must file the American tax return annually and pay tax on his worldwide income in the USA. US citizens are subject to worldwide taxation.

As already described above, however, certain requirements must also be met by German or European emigrants. Furthermore, it can also be assumed that in the foreseeable future, the European countries will certainly follow suit in order to tax their citizens worldwide, regardless of the center of life or residence. This is only a question of time.

A PT's philosophy is based on the 3-flag theory, which most PTs have expanded to a 5-flag theory. Occasionally this can also be expanded into a 6 flag theory. I will now explain all 3 theories in detail so that you can adopt the version that works best for you.

**The Three Flags Theory:**

1. Assume citizenship of a country that imposes no or very low taxes on foreign income worldwide.

2. Do your worldwide business outside the country where you reside and outside the country of where you are a citizen.

3. Live in the countries where you can pursue and live your hobbies and lifestyle undisturbed. These countries should be outside the above two states of which you are a resident and citizen.

So the basis of this theory is that you use different countries and jurisdictions for your domicile, citizenship, business and leisure respectively, which cannot interfere with each other in case of a problem. For example, if you go bankrupt in Panama with your offshore company, only in Panama does anyone care. However, assaults on you personally outside Panama are very difficult and costly because you are domiciled in Monaco, for example, and are a citizen of the United Kingdom. You have your capital in custody in Singapore and Hong Kong and you play golf in the posh club of Puerto Banus in Spain.

**The Five Flags Theory:**

1. You have a passport and citizenship of a country that does not tax you or hardly taxes you on your foreign income.

2. You have your residence in a tax haven.

3. You establish your companies in low-tax countries or tax havens.

4. You invest your capital in very safe areas in this respect, such as Singapore or Hong Kong.

5. You spend your money on hobbies and lifestyle in more states.

In the meantime, some PTs have also adapted a sixth flag:

6. States in which you have registered your web servers and websites. Countries with very few rules and regulations or very high security requirements against the disclosure of information are recommended.

Also important to this theory is that the 5 or 6 flags should each be a different jurisdiction. So use a different state for each flag so that you end up operating from at least 5 or 6 states.

On the surface, PTs have some things in common with so-called global citizens in that they do not themselves subscribe to any particular nation. Many PTs closely align themselves with libertarian or anarchist schools of thought that advocate individual sovereignty and do not want to transfer sovereignty of individuals to nation-states.

**The PT strategy and practical experience**

You should take the first step by deregistering from your previous high tax country for the first time. And you do not move directly to a tax haven or a low-tax country, but first inconspicuously to a neighboring country such as the Netherlands, Belgium, UK, Austria, Italy etc.. From there, after a few months, you set off to your real destination. If you don't just migrate with a capital of millions and with a whole hundred workers, like Müller Milch, then you can disguise yourself quite inconspicuously with this step-by-step method.

From there, you then go to the state where you want to apply for permanent residency.

This should preferably be a tax haven or low tax country, such as Channel Islands, Monaco, Bahamas, Turks & Caicos, Paraguay, Dominican Republic, etc. You will then apply for permanent residency there.

Once you have established your permanent residence in a tax haven, go about establishing your offshore companies in the appropriate territories and for the appropriate purposes. Don't put all your eggs in one basket here and set up your companies in several different territories for a variety of ventures and purposes. That way, if something goes wrong with a business, it won't all go to waste at once!

Onassis also established a separate company for each of his oil tankers and did not manage all tankers under one company. The following territories are very suitable for this purpose: Hong Kong, Singapore, Belize, Malta and Mauritius.

When starting a company, always try to start your company without a trustee if possible. This way you won't have to rely on anyone and you will remain extremely flexible in your ventures. Most areas will offer you fiduciary directors and stock holders. This is fine as long as you can get a general power of attorney and move freely with it. However, in most cases, you are significantly limited with your company with a fiduciary, as they will not sign off on all of your desired business, as they do not want to be held liable at all if possible.

You can see for yourself how quickly and easily you have thus already established your first three flags. You have your citizenship, your tax-free residence and your tax-free companies! Now all you have to do is move your website to a server in Uruguay or New Zealand and fly to Honolulu to play golf.

If, on the other hand, you are looking for something more exotic and erotic, then take a trip to Thailand and the Philippines and then fly on to Singapore and Hong Kong to set up your account or make deposits or withdrawals.

**Own experience**

Surely there are other spots on earth than the ones mentioned here where you can settle. I myself have been resident in quite a few tax havens and can first tell you as much about what all tax havens have in common: namely that you always have something that doesn't suit you.

Mostly it was the inaccessibility that bothered me in some places. For example, on the small Channel island of Isle of Sark, which does not levy any taxes, or in Andorra. The Isle of Sark has no taxes at all and you could start and run hundreds of companies there without any problems. The record was broken by a trustee appointed by a London tax firm with a whopping 3,000 companies. Considering that the island had only 500 inhabitants and a few sheep, this is quite amazing. At the time, every allotment on the island was home to a mailbox headquarters with several hundred firms. The disadvantage was that to get to the island, you first had to fly to Guernsey or Jersey from London. Then you could get to the island from there by mail boat, or in the summer from Jersey by catamaran. The last ferry back was at 5 p.m., and then it was closing time.

The island had 3 hotels and 3 pubs and a few family restaurants. There were no street lights, no cars and it was like the Middle Ages. In stormy seas it could happen in winter that you had no boat at all for 2 or 3 days to cross to the next larger island. For a jet set from Monaco this would have been the absolute horror and this would probably have felt like Napoleon's banishment on Elba compared to a suite in the Palace Hotel! Rubber boots and umbrellas were more in style than patent leather shoes and a tuxedo. The millions were transported in a plastic bag and hidden between milk and cheese, instead of in a Gucci suitcase.

Things were not much better in Andorra. Already the journey there stretched incredibly long into the Pyrenees, no matter whether you arrived from the French side or the Spanish side towards Barcelona. The only reasonable alternative was a helicopter service from Barcelona directly to Andorra La Vella. After you had eaten your way through all the restaurants during the first weeks, you got so bored that you voluntarily wanted to go back to Barcelona!

And I fared even worse on the Turks & Caicos Islands, which is the next island chain after the Bahamas. They have infinite turquoise water, some vacation clubs and glorious sunshine, as well as a few island beauties and lots of drunken Canadian and American tourists. After 14 days you start to get your first depression, after four weeks you have not only sunstroke but also island fever and after eight weeks- at the latest- you urgently need to get on a plane that will transport you back to a metropolis!

As I said, these views are very subjective and vary from person to person, so you should always discover and explore your own paradise!

In addition, you have to pay attention to the fact that you should not simply buy a plot of land in Paraguay or in the African bush without knowing who lives in your neighborhood. If an extreme crisis should occur, in which the local population is also threatened by hunger or chaos, you as the only foreigner will be the easy and first target of an attack. You should therefore make sure that you live in a community where at least locals and your own ethnic group already live together and you are not the only exotic one there.

**The German Foreign Tax Act**

When migrating abroad, it is imperative that you comply with this law and, as an entrepreneur, be sure to discuss your departure with a tax firm with legal counsel accordingly.

It is therefore essential that you observe the German Foreign Tax Act when you officially emigrate. In §6 "Taxation of capital gains" it is explained why a move out of the German tax territory can be expensive. In particular, this concerns entrepreneurs with corporations (e.g. GmbHs), which the state does not want to let go so easily.

Example: An entrepreneur makes an average profit of € 100,000 over the past 3 years. His company has unlimited tax liability and is therefore assessed in the country of residence at a tax rate of 30% (15% corporate income tax and 15% trade tax).

The tax authorities take the 100,000 € profit times 13.75 for a departure, which means that the entrepreneur has to pay tax on 1,375,000 € fictitious profit when leaving Germany. He pays tax on 60% of this sum, which is € 810,000. At a personal tax rate of 30%, you must pay € 243,000 in taxes on the fictitious profit. The emphasis here is on the word fictitious, since this assumed profit did not actually arise.

It is to be expected that in the coming years, the regulations in force will be tightened more and more as revenues are lost in the major industrialized countries.

The state does not like to see the elite leave, as they are needed to pay the taxes.

In this context, I would like to point out that there are still elegant ways to circumvent this taxation of fictitious (i.e. non-real) income.

I recommend a German contact who has a suitable German tax firm at hand. Just write to them:

STB-Consultings@protonmail.com

# TAX HAVEN

**What is a tax haven?**

A tax haven is a country in which the taxation of that country is exploited by foreigners or foreign companies on advantageous terms in order to reduce the tax burden in the actual home country.

The term "tax haven" is not firmly defined. There is no limit that can be set in absolute terms as to when a country is or is not a tax haven. Basically, any country can be a tax haven if the general conditions are right for a person or company. According to rarer criteria, Germany and the USA, for example, are also considered to be such. This refers to the fact that due to the huge number of laws and regulations especially in the tax area in these countries a vast amount of partly little known completely legal structuring possibilities exist. If you are interested, you can also contact my German contact here:

STB-Consultings@protonmail.com

So it is not only countries that levy particularly low taxes on certain types of income that are considered tax havens. A popular form of tax evasion, for example, is also the "parking" of funds in countries that hide these sums from the domestic tax authorities.

## The blacklists of tax evaders

In 2017, the European Union drew up a blacklist of 19 countries that they consider to be tax havens.

However, this list never came into force. After numerous objections and deletions, this list was whittled down to include only 5 countries at the end of 2018. In February 2019, the European Commission adopted a new list of third countries, now comprising 23 countries, which was again cut to about half in February 2020. Often criticized here are the justifications for the non-inclusions in the list: For example, Turkey was once again granted a deferral for "political reasons." The fact that the Cayman Islands were never on the list before seems even stranger. Before Brexit, they were considered an EU territory and therefore, by definition, could not be listed.

The FATF (Financial Action Task Force on Money Laundering) is an association of the European Union, the Gulf Cooperation Council and 38 individual countries, including China, Russia and the USA. The FATF blacklist is considered one of the most internationally recognized and has the highest weight next to the EU list.

Below I list the most common countries that are used by various companies and individuals as low-tax countries or tax havens for company formations or as a place of residence. Please note the legend at the end of the table:

| Name of the country | Oxfam | FATF | EU | IWF | CBI | FSI Rank |
|---|---|---|---|---|---|---|
| Trinidad und Tobago | X | X | X | | | 104 |
| Samoa | | | X | | | 79 |
| Seychellen | | | X | | X | 75 |
| Vanuatu | X | | X | | X | 65 |
| Panama | | | X | | | 12 |
| Kaimaninseln | X | | X | X | | 3 |
| Jungferninseln (US) | X | | X | | | |
| Oman | X | | X | | | |
| Palau | X | | X | | | |
| Guam | X | | X | | | |
| Fidschi | | | X | | | |
| Amerikanisch Samoa | | | X | | | |
| St. Lucia | | | | | X | 107 |
| Nauru | X | | | | | 105 |
| Botswana | | X | | | | 100 |
| Mazedonien | X | | | | | 99 |
| Grenada | | | | | X | 98 |
| Cookinseln | X | | | | | 97 |
| Montenegro | X | | | | | 96 |

| Name of the country | Oxfam | FATF | EU | IWF | CBI | FSI Rank |
|---|---|---|---|---|---|---|
| Antigua und Barbuda | X | | | | X | 95 |
| Dominica | | | | | X | 93 |
| Ghana | | X | | | | 92 |
| Turks und Caicosinseln | | | | | X | 84 |
| Curaçao | X | | | | | 82 |
| Gibraltar | X | | | | | 81 |
| Aruba | X | | | | | 67 |
| Anguilla | X | | | | | 56 |
| Mauritius | X | | | | | 49 |
| Barbados | | | | | X | 48 |
| Marshallinseln | X | | | | | 39 |
| Bermuda | X | | | X | | 36 |
| Malaysia | | | | | X | 31 |
| Irland | X | | | X | | 26 |
| Zypern | | | | | X | 24 |
| Kanada | X | | | | | 21 |
| Malta | X | | | | X | 20 |
| Bahamas | X | X | | | X | 19 |
| Jersey | X | | | | | 18 |

| Name of the country | Oxfam | FATF | EU | IWF | CBI | FSI Rank |
|---|---|---|---|---|---|---|
| Bahrain | X | | | | X | 17 |
| Jungferninseln (UK) | X | | | X | | 16 |
| Thailand | | | | | | 15 |
| Niederlande | X | | | X | | 14 |
| Japan | | | | | | 13 |
| Libanon | | | | | | 11 |
| Guernsey | | | | | | 10 |
| Arabische Emirate | X | | | | X | 9 |
| Taiwan | X | | | | | 8 |
| Deutschland | | | | | | 7 |
| Luxemburg | X | | | X | | 6 |
| Singapur | X | | | X | | 5 |
| Hongkong | X | | | X | | 4 |
| USA | | | | | | 2 |
| Schweiz | X | | | | | 1 |
| Serbien | X | X | | | | |
| Katar | | | | | X | |
| St. Kitts und Nevis | | | | | X | |
| Bosnien Herzegowina | X | | | | | |

| Name of the country | Oxfam | FATF | EU | IWF | CBI FSI Rank |
|---|---|---|---|---|---|
| Niue | X | | | | |
| Sri Lanka | | X | | | |
| Jemen | | X | | | |
| Tunesien | | X | | | |
| Syrien | | X | | | |
| Pakistan | | X | | | |
| Iran | | X | | | |
| Äthiopien | | X | | | |
| Nordkorea | | X | | | |
| Kambodscha | | X | | | |
| Färöer-Inseln | X | | | | |
| Grönland | X | | | | |
| Albanien | X | | | | |

**Explanation of each list in the table above:**

Oxfam: The "Corporate Tax Havens" List of the most important NGOs

FATF:  List of the Financial Action Task Force on Money Laundering

EU:  The last adopted list of the EU from February 2020.

IMF:  International Monetary Fund blacklist

CBI: OECD list of countries where citizenship can be bought through investment.

FSI: The "Financial Secrecy Index", which indicates in which countries money can be hidden from other countries by having corresponding laws that either strongly emphasize banking secrecy and/or limit the "willingness to disclose" of the authorities to a minimum vis-à-vis other countries.

It would go far beyond the scope of this article to deal with each tax area individually. I leave this to my readers.

You can "google" each individual country and find out the relevant information and tax framework for each country including income tax, which is 0 for some countries. Therefore, it is not possible to make a blanket statement about which are the best tax havens, as this depends individually on the needs of each user and their demands and quality of life and business. Nevertheless, I would like to provide you with detailed information at least for three of the countries most used for offshore business:

These are Dubai, Singapore, Hong Kong and England.

For more information on various low-tax countries, see the "Second Passport" chapter in this book.

**Your Company and Residency in Dubai:**

Dubai is the preferred location for business in the UAE. Since 2000, Dubai has witnessed incredible growth throughout all sectors of its diverse economy and its Government is constantly working to improve its commercial transparency and introduce dynamic regulations that aid the formation of small and medium enterprises. Setting up a company in Dubai is now one of the most attractive options for entrepreneurs in the UAE.

With its central geographic location between Asian and European markets, Dubai has established itself as an internationally recognized trading hub.

What makes company formation in Dubai so attractive, is the features of its free zones. Dubai's many free zones have enabled the United Arab Emirates to attract more foreign investment as free zones adhere to unique laws regarding ownership, taxation and labor. Unlike businesses in the rest of Dubai, which require at least 51% ownership by a UAE national, free zone businesses can have 100% foreign ownership.

**Why set up a business in Dubai?**

Here are some of the key advantages to setting up a company in Dubai:

The UAE is focused on helping businesses to succeed. The government has invested significantly in business development and support over the years. This is especially evident in the free zones – areas where foreign entrepreneurs can set up a business without requiring an UAE sponsor. Starting a business in a Dubai free zone is efficient and cost effective. You can operate with freedom, plus benefit from the multiple amenities, facilities and networking opportunities on offer.

Another reason why forming a company is Dubai is attractive is that fact it is perfectly situated for both onshore and offshore companies. It links the east and the west, and is a world-leader in terms of international trade. It's also well-connected, with two international airports, two commercial ports, plus excellent overland transport links.

Dubai is politically stable and is a global trailblazer in terms of business and commerce. To encourage foreign investment, the government has made it incredibly straightforward, with the correct guidance, to set up a company in Dubai, and there are numerous tax incentives too.

Dubai offers a good working environment, and a great lifestyle for residents too. Once you've set up a company here, you can easily apply for a residency visa, which allows you to rent property, purchase vehicles, and travel without restriction. You'll also find that there's plenty to see and do in the UAE, with activities for all the family.

## Things to consider when you set up a company in Dubai

### Do you need a UAE national to act as a sponsor?

If you're setting up a company in one of Dubai's free zones, you won't require a local sponsor (a UAE national who acts as a partner, owning 51% of the company). However, if you're setting up an onshore business, a sponsor is required. Please note that sponsors will also charge an annual fee. However, also the structure will be set up that you have 100% control over your company onshore Dubai even you need a sponsor.

### What location works best for you?

There are numerous location options when setting up a business in Dubai.

Operating in one of Dubai's free zones benefits many businesses, in a variety of different sectors. However, if you need to be in the center of the city (e.g. if you run a retail company), setting up in a free zone might not be the best option. There are many other geographical considerations too. For example, does your business need to be near one of the ports, or one of the airports? Is it B2B or B2C? Are there good transport links nearby? We will consider these important questions before advising where to locate your company.

**What sort of set-up works best for you?**

There are three different types of business set-up in Dubai, and each offer different advantages. The options are:

**Offshore.** An offshore company can't trade in UAE, so you won't be entitled to a visa. However, 100% foreign ownership is permissible.

**Free zone.** The situation is the same as it is for offshore, but you can apply for a visa.

**Onshore.** Dubai Mainland Company Requirements mean you must obtain a DED license, and a local partner must own 51% of the company. This is the right option if you plan to open a shop in the center of Dubai selling clothing, for example.

**Are you eligible for a visa?**

If you want to operate an onshore business in Dubai, you'll need to have a visa for both you and your staff. These aren't difficult to obtain, but be aware that you'll need to fulfill certain criteria in order to be eligible. The authorities will want to know details about your business operations, who the investors are, and how large your premises are (among other things). To get a visa, you'll also need to provide documents like your passport, proof of address, and a letter from your sponsor (if you've got one).

## What assistance do you need?

Most businesses in Dubai choose to work with a specialist agency. These agencies have the advantage of being familiar with the process of setting up a company in your chosen country. Charterhouse Lombard are on hand to help with starting a business in Dubai, either in one of the free zones, or another location and assist with residence visa processing

## What sort of office?

Identify what sort of premises you require, and whether anything suitable is available. You'll need to consider your budget, and think about the future too (e.g. what options you'll have if you need to upscale your business).

## What license do you need?

Starting a business in Dubai requires a license. There are several different license categories in Dubai. Weigh up your options carefully, as you don't want to select a license that limits your business. This is something that an advisory agency can assist with.

**Which bank will you use?**

There are a lot of options in Dubai, and choosing the right bank isn't just a matter of selecting the one with the best reputation. Find out what charges are involved, and if the bank places any limitations on your business activities. Remember that you're looking for a bank that allows you to grow without restriction.

**Benefits of setting up a company in a UAE Free Zone**

There are a number of advantages to freezone company formation in the UAE. Here are just a few:
- Directors, shareholders and employees can get RESIDENCY VISAS IN THE UAE
- 100% foreign ownership is permitted – you won't need a local sponsor
- Exemption from taxes (corporate and personal income)
- Repatriation of capital and profits
- No currency restrictions
- Networking opportunities
- Infrastructure established to help businesses to thrive
- Wide range of licensable business activities
- Convenient locations (close to airports, ports, main roads etc.)
- Support for start-ups and smaller companies

- Liberal policies and local business laws
- 100% free fund transfers

**A guide to the Free Zones**

There are more than 37 free zones operating in the UAE, each with their own special tax, customs and imports regimes.

The following are the most notable free zones in the UAE:

**International Free zone Authority Companies**

The International Free Zone Authority (IFZA) provides fast processing times, tax exemption and 100% repatriation of foreign capital. The free zone is highly cost-effective and efficient with a variety of consultancy services and trading activities available for your License.

**Dubai South Free Zone** offer companies a 100% tax-free operation, no corporation tax, competitive rates and more.

**DMCC Free Zone**

This free zone has been awarded the Financial Times' fDi Magazine 'Global Free Zone of the Year' in 2015, 2016, 2017 and 2018 with 170 new companies making the move every month. The Free zone offers

0% personal and corporate income for 50 years, with no restrictions on remittance payments back to home territories.

### Fujairah Free Zone Companies

This Free Zone provides rapid processing times, total exemption from tax and 100% repatriation of foreign capital. It has a wide range of consultancy, services and trading activities available for your License. The free zone is highly cost-effective and efficient.

**RAK Free Zone Companies** is gaining a global reputation; with companies from across Europe, North America, Middle East and Asia bringing their business to RAKEZ, this free trade zone has now registered more than 13,000 companies worldwide.

### SHAMS Free Zone Comp

This free zone provides 0% corporate tax for 50 years, 0% import and export duties, full foreign ownership, free transfer of funds and complete repatriation of all capital and profits. SHAMS is the third largest free zone in the UAE and the hub for media and creative industries.

## Jebel Ali Free Zone (Dubai) Companies

Jebel Ali is DP World's flagship free zone, and the largest free zone in the world. It caters for businesses in the trading, logistics and industrial sectors. As the name suggests, it's located in the Jebel Ali district in the west of Dubai, close to the Abu Dhabi border. There are currently around 7,000 businesses in residence here; 100 of which are Fortune Global 500 enterprises.

## Dubai Knowledge Park Companies

Dubai Knowledge Park caters for businesses in HR, personal development and training. It was established in 2003, and currently houses over 400 registered companies. Partners include Michigan State University and the University of Wollongong, Dubai.

## Dubai Internet City Companies

Dubai Internet City offers support for those involved with communication and the internet. It was established in 2000, and now has over 1,400 businesses operating within it. Many global enterprises are situated here, including Microsoft, Canon, Siemens and Dell.

## How to register a company in one of the Free Zones?

Here's a quick run-through of what's involved:

Establish what sort of company you want to set up.

You'll need to declare the nature of your business, and which free zone you want to establish yourself in. Bear in mind that a capital requirement may be in place – this depends on which free zone you choose.

## Select your name.

When registering your company, you'll need to select a name. Be warned – a few words may be forbidden, and other restrictions may be in place (though these are fairly limited in the UAE).

## Get your business licence.

Each company License must have at least one specific activity listed – here is a wide range to choose from. There are several different licences available in the UAE, and which one you choose will depend entirely on what sort of business you'll be running. Please note that in certain cases you will require some supporting documents when applying.

**Find the right premises.**

Most free zones have a wide range of offices and workplaces to choose from, which are available to either purchase or lease. Offices are not required in all instances.

**Get approved.**

After you've submitted your registration, you'll need to wait for the initial approval from the relevant authorities. Turnaround is usually swift, so you won't have to wait for long.

**Formally register your company.**

Once we've received approval, we can register your business and obtain your license.

**Common Free Zone Questions**

**What documents will you need?**

This varies, depending on the nature of your business. At the very least, you'll require a copy of your passport and UAE visa or entry stamp, one proof of address (less than 3 months old), and our company application form.

### Is it better to set up in a free zone than as an offshore venture?

If you require a residency visa, then a Free zone company is a must. Free zones offer numerous advantages. Some businesses view them as the best of both worlds, as free zone companies are essentially onshore ventures with offshore features. However, they can be more expensive to set up.

### How many residency visas can you obtain?

This depends on visa allocation at the time of incorporation and the size of your premises. Rules vary from freezone to freezone.

### Are your business activities confidential?

Free zones offer high levels of confidentiality for their businesses. No information is available on the public record.

### What licences are on offer?

There are a range of licences to choose from in UAE. These include:
- The trading / commercial license
- The consultancy license

- The general trading license
- The industrial license
- The service license
- The warehousing license
- The manufacturing license

**What is a free zone visa?**

The UAE's free zones offer businesses a lot of benefits. There are over 45 free zones in total, and many offer tax exemptions for companies that operate within them, plus 100% foreign ownership.

However, having the right visa is important in order to operate your company effectively. The visa assists you with opening a company bank account, obtaining a local UAE phone number and many other business activities.

Free zone visas can be obtained from the Immigration Department (not the Ministry of Labour), and are valid for three years. After this time, you'll need to renew the visa, in order to continue living and working in the country.

## How to get your UAE free zone visa

The process for gaining a free zone visa is as follows:
1. Apply for Entry Permit
2. Entry permit received client has 60 days to fly to Dubai with said permit.
3. Entry permit stamped on arrival in Dubai
4. Collect entry permit and original passport from client and get medical fitness report and emirates Identity card application typed at typing Centre.
5. Collect client and take for medical test.
6. Receive medical fitness report confirmation.
7. Collect client and take for emirates ID card biometrics.
8. Process basic medical insurance certificate.
9. Submit passport, medical result, emirates iD process confirmation and copy of basic medical insurance to freezone.
10. Visa stamped in passport.
11. Collect passport from freezone and deliver to client.
12. Client emirates identity card delivered to our P.O. Box - collect and deliver to client.
13. Process complete.

The UAE boasts some of the best amenities and infrastructure in the world. For example, UAE residents have access to outstanding healthcare facilities in private hospitals and sophisticated clinics. Also, there is a wide range of internationally accredited private schools offering English language education from nursery to primary school and through to high school. Many of the schools in Dubai and Abu Dhabi follow the UK schooling system.

Dubai also has one of the world's leading offshore business sectors with the Dubai International Financial Centre. This prestigious free zone offers a range of financial benefits such as zero corporate, personal, import and export taxes. In addition, the Dubai free zone offers access to major international banks.

### How to Get a Residency in the UAE?

There are six principal ways for foreigners to get a UAE residency permit. The most popular ways to become a resident are through employment or incorporating a company. However, residency in the UAE is also possible by purchasing real estate, studying, being married to a UAE resident, or retiring.

### Incorporating Your Company in the UAE

### Who can apply?

One of the easiest ways to get UAE residency is to apply as an investor or shareholder.

**How long does it take?**

It takes between two and eight weeks to incorporate a company in the UAE, depending on whether it's an offshore company or a limited liability company (LLC).

**Is there any regulation for businesses?**

All incorporated companies must meet the relevant Economic Substance Regulations in the Emirate.

**How long is residency valid?**

Investors who gain UAE residency get a permit that is valid for three years.

**As a Family Member of UAE Resident or National**

**Who can apply?**

Family members of employers and employees in the UAE with a valid residency permit can apply for residency. To be eligible, the UAE resident or national must earn at least AED 4,000 or AED 3,000 plus accommodation.

**Required documents**

The necessary documents to apply for residency as a family member of UAE resident or national include the following:
- Copies of passports and passport-size photos
- Medical clearance of all applicants over 18 years of age
- Copy of the UAE resident or national's employment contract
- Certificate of earnings
- Legalised marriage certificate
- Registered tenancy contract
- Copy of a recent utility bill

**How long does it take?**

It takes between ten and 15 days to process documents for a family residence permit in the UAE

**Retirement**

**Who can apply?**

Any retired person over 55 years of age can apply for a long-term residency permit. The eligibility requirements are as follows:
- Investment in a property worth over AED 2 million
- Savings of over AED 1 million

- An active income of at least AED 20,000

**Required documents**

To prove financial stability, retirees applying for UAE residency should show bank statements from the previous six months, a copy of the property title deed, and the usual documents for residency permit applications. Additionally, it is required to show a valid health insurance policy.

**How long does it take?**

It can take up to two weeks to process a UAE Retirement Residency application.

**How long does residency valid?**

The UAE residency permit for retirees lasts for five years.

## Employment Contract

### What kind of company?

You can apply for residency in the UAE if you plan to work in a company based in the Emirates. Additionally, applying for a residency is essential if you want to work in the Emirati government.

### How long does it take?

It takes two to three weeks to process the initial work entry permit. This document is valid for two months, during which time you should apply for residency.

### Required documents?

The necessary documents for working in the UAE include the following:
- An employment contract or signed offer letter
- Health insurance and medical fitness certificate
- Copy of passport
- Copy of the company's establishment card

## SET UP COSTS FOR RESIDENCY AND COMPANY

The average fee what is involved for forming your UAE company with all documentations, licenses, sponsors ect. and applying for a 3 years residency permit will be between 5.000 USD and 7.000 USD. You have yearly fees for license, office and sponsor of your company.

That means with an amount under 10.000 USD you can establish your own tax free residency in the UAE and operate your own legal tax free company in a nice and safe environment!

**Facts on company formation in Hong Kong:**

Hong Kong is still the gateway for market access to China and Asia, independent, open to the movement of goods and services, free trade center for goods, services of all kinds and especially for foreign exchange.

The Private Limited Company is the most popular legal form of company in Hong Kong and is chosen almost without exception by all foreign companies based in Hong Kong. Despite the current turmoil, Hong Kong will nevertheless remain an important and secure financial center for the next 5-10 years.

The minimum legal requirements for establishing a limited company in Hong Kong are:

- Share capital of HKD 10,000 which, however, does not have to be fully paid in.
- A company charter, which is usually very broad and regulates the powers of the directors and the business purpose of the company. Business purpose can be manufacturing and distribution, trade or in import/export and services of all kinds.
- Two shareholders as well as two directors; shareholders and directors may be identical (and often are in the case of small companies) and may be legal entities as well as natural persons, who need not be residents of Hong Kong.

- A Company Secretary, who must be a Hong Kong resident and who is responsible for, among other things, reporting to the Registrar of Companies.

**Taxes in Hong Kong:**

Hong Kong enjoys a special position in relation to China due to its special status, which is governed by the CEPA agreement.

The tax rate on corporate profits is 17.5%. In practice, however, it is often considerably lower, as all interest income from bank deposits **and profits earned abroad or in the People's Republic of China** are **completely tax-free in Hong Kong.** Furthermore, the legal regulations for the tax deductibility of expenses and costs are very generous. This alone makes the lack of a double taxation agreement between the Special Administrative Region of Hong Kong and Germany virtually irrelevant in practice. There are no sales or value-added taxes in Hong Kong. Import duties are generally only levied on spirits, tobacco products, gasoline and diesel fuel, and motor vehicles.

**Facts on company formation in Singapore:**

Type of company used:
Private Limited Company (Pte Ltd)
- Secretary required: Yes

- Capital stock requirement: No capital stock required (1 SGD)
- Renewal date: anniversary date of the company / every year publicly
- Basis of the legal system: Common law
- Minimum number of directors / shareholders:
  At least    1 director / 1 shareholder
  One of the directors must be resident in Singapore.
- Bearer shares are not permitted.

**Accessible information concerning the management:**

The names of the directors and shareholders appear in the register and are publicly available.

**Confidentiality:**

Singapore offers a high level of anonymity and privacy protection.

**Accounting obligation:**

Yes. Annual reports must be submitted.

**Legislation:**

Singapore Companies Act 1963.

**Default currency:**

SGD- Singapore Dollar

**Stability:**

Singapore is an extremely stable state and enjoys an excellent reputation.

**Communication:**

Very good news connections

**Time zone:**

Favorable time zone: GMT+8

**Taxation:**

- 17% above SGD 300,000, 8.5% below
- No taxes on profits generated abroad or on income derived from financial assets.

**The English (UK) Limited Company/ Ltd.**

The UK Limited Company is certainly the optimal company construction in the whole of Europe. A thoroughbred company like a limited liability company (GmbH), which is recognized and capable of doing business everywhere. But it is still different compared to other companies. The UK Limited Company does not know any liability, no publicity obligations and no limitation of liability. Properly used, new sources of money can be tapped and bank or supply credits can become a common financial instrument. By splitting the company into a holding company and an operating company, it also offers reliable protection against the risk of bankruptcy or divorce. Advantages upon advantages. This book explains the legal provisions and requirements you need to be aware of to set up a UK Limited.

**Legal forms of a limited company**

The *Limited Company* is a company under private law and therefore a legal entity. It is a corporation whose share capital is divided into shares. The liability of the shareholders is limited to this capital. The shares are transferable. The following types of companies exist in the United Kingdom:

**Private Company limited By Shares**

The *private company limited by shares* is the form of company used for small and medium-sized enterprises and thus the most widespread form of corporation in the United Kingdom. The difference to the *public limited company* is that the *private company limited by shares* may not offer shares to the public and is therefore not traded on the stock exchange. When publications refer to the *limited* or *limited company,* it is this form of company they are talking about. The name of the company must always contain an addition identifying the legal form. The additions *Limited* or the abbreviation *Ltd* are used.

For Welsh companies, the addition *Cyfyngedig* or the abbreviation *Cyf* can be used alternatively.

### Private company limited by guarantee

In the case of the *private company limited by guarantee*, in contrast to the usual form of corporation, no share capital is formed, but the owners issue a guarantee to be liable for the company's liabilities up to a certain amount in the event of the company's insolvency. It is a special form often applied to non-profit companies that need to act as a legal entity. These include clubs, student bodies, sports associations (for example, the PGA European Tour), cooperatives, non-governmental organizations or charities (for example, Oxfam). The name of the company must contain the same suffix as the *private company limited by share.*

### Private unlimited company

The *private unlimited company* is a company that can issue shares, but is not obliged to do so. It is a special form of the corporation, in which however all partners have unlimited liability, whereby these can be natural or legal persons. It is used when the partners are to have unlimited liability, but the company must act as a separate legal entity. The name of the company must in each case contain the addition *Unlimited*, which characterizes the legal form.

**Public limited company**

The *public limited company* is the usual corporate form for larger, often listed stock corporations. Since it can offer its shares to the public or have them traded on the stock exchange, it is subject to stricter reporting and notification requirements. In addition, it requires a company secretary, who must meet certain requirements (for example, they must be a certified accountant or a certified attorney-at-law). The company's name must in each case use an addition indicating the legal form *public limited company* or the abbreviation *PLC.* For Welsh companies, the addition *Cwmni Cyfyngedig Cyhoeddus* or the abbreviation *CCC* may be used alternatively.

In principle, all worldwide profits of the British corporation must be taxed in the United Kingdom. Due to a large number of double taxation agreements, for example with Germany, there are corresponding exceptions. Even if the head office of the limited company is not located in the United Kingdom, the tax return must be prepared in accordance with British regulations. However, if the company operates exclusively in Germany, for example, it can be exempted from the British tax return obligation and thus also from the tax liability. Corporation tax and, if applicable, value added tax (VAT) must be paid. Dividends paid are taxable at the personal income tax rate if the shareholder is resident in the UK. The following are the tax rates for corporation tax in the United Kingdom as of 2008.

| Profit | Tax rate | Remarks |
| --- | --- | --- |
| up to 300 000 £ | 21 % | Tax rate for small companies (small companies rate) |
| 300 000 £ up to 1 500 000 £ | 21 %-28 % | Transition area (Marginal relief) |
| from 1 500 000 £ | 28 % | Normal tax rate (Main rate) |

Note upcoming change in the context of the UK leaving the EU (BREXIT). At the completion of this book, many issues are still open in this area and need to be verified.

**Double taxation agreement**

*What is a double taxation treaty?*

A double taxation agreement is a treaty under international law aimed at avoiding double taxation. An agreement can be reached between two states (bilateral) or between several states (multilateral). In this case, a uniform right of taxation is negotiated should a tax object assume a cross-border dimension. In addition, the focus is on combating tax evasion with political cooperation.

*What is the purpose of the double taxation agreement?*

A tax conflict may arise when a legal entity generates income in two states.

For example, a company makes a profit abroad that is to be offset domestically. In this case, both states have the right to levy taxes. This leads to double taxation, which the double taxation treaty is designed to avoid. The agreement is subject to principles that must be followed in the practice of international tax law. Here, the country of residence principle stipulates that a legal entity is liable to tax in the country in which it has its main residence. This is opposed by the source country principle. Accordingly, a legal entity is liable to tax in the country in which it generates its income. A prerequisite is the world income principle, according to which world income may only be taxed once. This is supplemented by the territoriality principle, according to which income is taxed in the territory in which it was earned. Which principles are applied to what extent is regulated by internal laws.

**Annotation:**

There is really nothing new to add to the "Panama Papers" scandal. Keep your hands off Switzerland, Austria and tax havens like Panama without having emigrated to a low tax country yourself. Please also note that WITHOUT RESIDENCE in Germany you are liable to pay taxes where you have your main residence. If this is in a low tax country or directly in a tax haven, nobody cares anyway if you have an offshore company, no matter in which jurisdiction it is located, because you do not pay tax at your domicile! The construct only becomes illegal if you have a primary residence in a high tax jurisdiction, but make profits through your offshore company that you then do not pay tax on at your primary residence or do not declare on your tax return. If you pay tax on this income, this construct is also perfectly legal.

Likewise, it is legal to own an offshore company and do business with it worldwide. If you do not make a profit distribution to yourself, then there is simply also nothing to pay tax on, because you have received nothing and the company itself is only taxable where it is resident and registered. Basic tenor here as well: If your circumstances allow it, deregister from your tax desert. Better today than tomorrow!

If, on the other hand, you wish to remain in Germany, there are also many ways to save taxes there. I have already given you the relevant contact address for this in the previous section.

**9 facts about the death of the classic offshore company**

**Tempi passati: The glorious era of the notorious zero-tax company on a Caribbean island has been a thing of the past**

**forever since 2016 at the latest. What are the consequences? What alternatives are there?**

Are you thinking of setting up an offshore company in Hong Kong, Singapore, Dubai, the British Virgin Islands (BVI), the Seychelles, the Bahamas, Gibraltar, Belize, Mauritius, Jersey, the Isle of Man, St Vincent or one of the other relevant tax havens?

Did you know that all the countries mentioned here (and around 100 others) signed an agreement on the automatic exchange of information with your tax office back in 2014, which came into force on 01.01.2016?

In the past, the names of the various offshore domicile states, which are as melodious as they are exotic, were synonymous with extremely low (or mostly no) corporate taxes, anonymity and entrepreneurial freedom.

Those who founded an International Business Company (IBC) or another common offshore legal form were often able to channel funds discreetly past the tax authorities. From the point of view of the home tax office, this was highly problematic, but the founder could, as is well known, rely on the secrecy of all parties involved.

For decades, the governments of these tax havens in particular successfully fought tooth and nail against handing over data on the backers and beneficiaries of offshore companies to interested tax authorities in various high-tax countries - after all, the existence of their mostly impoverished states depended to a large extent on the need for secrecy on the part of foreign offshore founders.

But that has changed dramatically in the meantime and any form of banking secrecy, confidentiality and anonymity is finally over and done with.

The classic offshore company is effectively dead and cannot be revived.

In the following, we have compiled 9 facts about widespread offshore structures, which should illustrate the current situation and point out possible solutions.

- Fact 1: Thanks to the OECD CRS, the anonymity of offshore companies is now a thing of the past worldwide.
- Fact 2: Start-up agencies have no idea about international tax law
- Fact 3: Trust models and foundations are passé
- Fact 4: From your high-tax country of residence, tax-optimized operation of an offshore company is not possible
- Fact 5: A foreign company must be able to demonstrate substance
- Fact 6: The administrative burden for offshore companies increases significantly
- Fact 7: Opening an account for an offshore company is a complicated and lengthy process
- Fact 8: For whom the use of an offshore company is still harmless today

- Fact 9: There are legal and equally tax-efficient onshore alternatives to offshore companies

**Fact 1: Thanks to the OECD CRS, the anonymity of offshore companies is now a thing of the past worldwide.**

We are currently witnessing the most significant changes in international tax law in 30 years. Both the OECD Common Reporting Standard (CRS) and the OECD BEPS (Base Erosion and Profit Shifting) project have far-reaching consequences for the use of offshore companies.

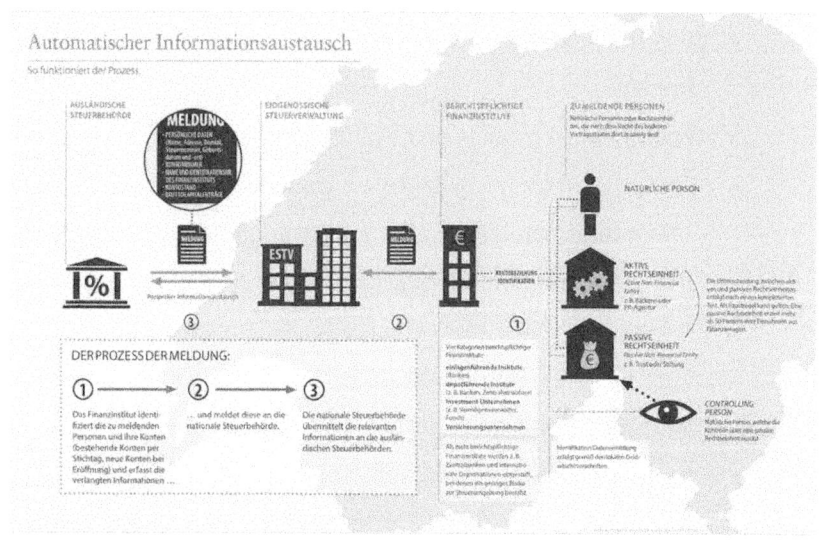

How the automatic exchange of information works

CRS is already implemented and active.

OECD CRS results in banks in more than 100 countries (including all offshore financial centers including Hong Kong, Dubai, Liechtenstein, Cayman Islands, etc.) automatically exchanging information with the tax authorities of foreign account holders with immediate effect.

The exchange of information does not stop at company accounts. If you own 20% or more of the shares in a foreign company, you will also be subject to the exchange of information.

CRS was implemented in stages until 2018. Existing accounts will also be affected by the exchange of information.

Even if the account was closed before the country-specific CRS implementation date, it can be queried as part of so-called "group queries".

A tax authority can request a list of certain accounts from the authorities of another country - e.g. accounts of all German citizens with cash assets exceeding €100,000 whose account has existed for more than 10 years.

**Fact 2: Start-up agencies have no idea about international tax law**

You will continue to find plenty of offers on the Internet for the formation and management of offshore companies in all kinds of countries. A simple Google search is enough to come across countless relevant incorporation agencies.

Most start-up agencies have no idea of what is "going on". They do not even begin to understand the tax implications of current global initiatives such as OECD CRS. The start-up agencies also continue to assume that there will always be one other state that "does not participate". After all, that has always been the case. But this is precisely what has changed.

The fact that the founder is exposed to considerable tax risks here is taken lightly by the start-up agency. Who would want to admit that their own product could have criminal consequences for the buyer, including imprisonment?

Instead of warning the founder and pointing out the tax risks, and even advising him against founding a company, they continue to sell eagerly. In keeping with the motto: After us the deluge!

And when the chips have fallen, the blame is always shifted to the banks that "screwed up."

*As a client, you have to face reality: Establishing a foreign company is a complex tax issue. Don't let yourself be talked into anything. Put yourself in the hands of an experienced expert who will advise you against the foreign project rather than expose you to an unnecessarily high risk.*

Here is another graphic on how the automatic exchange of information works:

**So funktioniert der automatische Informationsaustausch (AIA)**

Am AIA nehmen weltweit über 90 Länder teil. Er soll sicherstellen, dass die Banken nur versteuertes Geld verwalten

Diese Daten werden übermittelt
Name, Adresse, Domizil
Steuernummer
Geburtsdatum
Geburtsort
Kontonummer
Name und Identifikationsnummer der Bank
Kontostand am Ende des Jahres
Bruttokapitalerträge

Schweizer Bank — Ausländische Kunden bringen ihr Geld auf eine Schweizer Bank
Die Bank liefert einmal jährlich Daten über die ausländischen Kunden an die Schweizer Steuerbehörden
Steuerbehörde — Diese gibt die Daten an das entsprechende Land weiter, sofern es am AIA teilnimmt und ein Abkommen mit der Schweiz hat
Steuerbehörde

TA-Grafik mtue / Quelle: Swissbanking.org

## Fact 3: Fiduciary models and foundations as a means of concealment are passé

If you think that OECD CRS can be evaded via a trustee or a foundation or trust, think again.

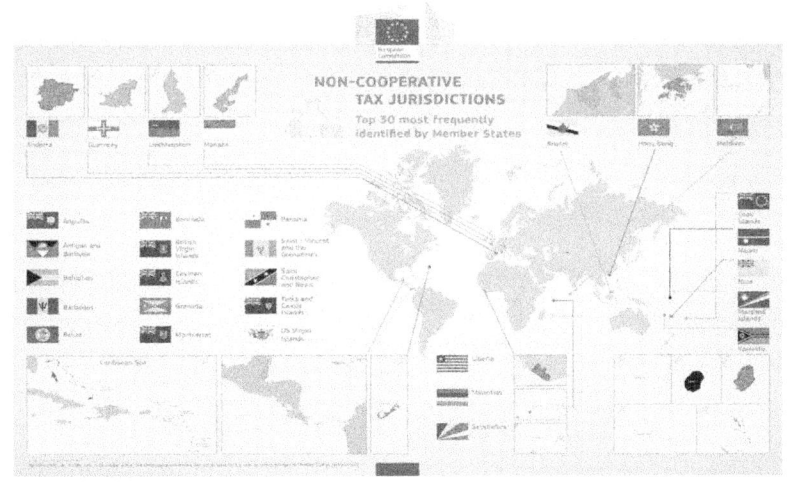

Non-cooperating tax havens as reported by EU governments

Professional fiduciaries such as tax advisors, attorneys, trust companies and fiduciaries are also required to participate in the exchange of information in most cases.

All foundations must disclose who their beneficiaries are. This is particularly true for foundations in Liechtenstein. As is well known, Liechtenstein has decided to take a pioneering role in matters of transparency and is now active on the front line as a "clarifier" - surpassed in zeal only by Switzerland, which has already published personal data of holders of various "black money accounts" in the newspaper.

And even if the trustee himself is not obliged to exchange information, then the account-holding bank must in any case disclose the fiduciary relationship. The bank will then make the corresponding report in the context of the exchange of information.

And what happens if a trustee conceals the fiduciary relationship from the bank? Since the trustee would be liable to prosecution and threatens to have his license revoked, it is not to be assumed that professional trustees will take this risk.

*You can no longer rely on trust structures to disguise the real beneficiaries in your offshore venture. There will be no more anonymity in the future. The design via trustees and foundations is obsolete in this respect as of now.*

**Fact 4: Tax-optimized operation of an offshore company is not possible from your country of residence**

It's nothing really new, but it's worth mentioning again at this point: if you live in one of the major industrialized nations, tax-optimized operation of an offshore company is impossible.

The world's leading tax havens

As I said, this has always been the case, but up to now, some owners of offshore companies have simply accepted the risk and speculated on not being discovered. Often enough, this strategy worked. But the exchange of information has put an end to this.

Most countries have laws on so-called "addition taxation". In Germany, this is part of the Foreign Tax Act. Other countries have so-called "CFC rules" or a "CFC regime" (CFC =Controlled Foreign Corporation).

The content of these tax regulations is always the same: If you live in State A and operate a corporation in State B, you must know that the corporation is probably also liable to tax in State A (the State of residence) - sometimes under drastically worse conditions than domestic corporations.

This is because the taxation of a corporation is based, among other things, on the place of management ("management and control") and the place where the services are rendered.

The double taxation agreements between states (DTAs) have a certain shielding effect and weaken some regulations in their effect. If there is no DTA (as is the case with all tax havens), this DTA shielding effect does not apply.

In addition, companies in low-tax countries are viewed with particular suspicion by the tax authorities of high-tax countries. As a result, it is theoretically perfectly legal to own an offshore company, but the country of residence can expect major negative tax effects. You may end up paying more taxes than if you register a simple trade or establish a company in your country of residence.

Only if you live in a state that does not have an "addition taxation" or CFC regime, the ownership of an offshore company makes sense and is still possible in a tax-optimized way.

*The offshore company is a tax trap if you set it up and operate it without precise planning and expert advice (and even then, in most cases, simply impossible). Setting up a company "just like that" and hoping not to be discovered is not a solution - especially not in times of automatic exchange of information.*

## Fact 5: A foreign company must be able to demonstrate substance

In 2012, the operators of the YouPorn Internet platform were targeted by the public prosecutor's office. Reason: A Regus Virtual Office is unfortunately not enough substance in the long run.

The reason for this was that parts of the website were externally managed by a company in Cyprus. In fact, however, the business was managed from Hamburg. According to the public prosecutor's office, the company in Cyprus was a letterbox company. The place of business management was Hamburg.

YouPorn founder Fabian Thylmann was only released on payment of a record bail of 10 million euros. The case involved evaded taxes in the millions.

The YouPorn example illustrates the problem that many foreign and offshore companies have: A lack of substance commercially established operating facility, staff and local management.

But as is unfortunately often the case, one's own comfort and quality of life seem to be more important than the necessities of international tax law. In addition, many of the people concerned are unfortunately frighteningly ignorant and negligent. In the long run, Hamburg is much more pleasant for many than Cyprus. The YouPorn employees probably had "no desire" to eke out an existence on an underdeveloped Mediterranean island. But is a prison stay in Hamburg really more pleasant?

The quality of life in Germany is outstanding compared to many other countries. But this quality of life comes at a price, and one of them is higher taxes. This is a relatively simple (and, at least from the state's point of view, very fair) calculation.

Presumably, YouPorn employees would have been persuaded to move to Cyprus by doubling their salaries. Perhaps the company's management didn't want to pay more and thus clearly saved on the wrong end.

Many founders of foreign and offshore companies are not willing, for reasons of convenience and comfort, to make the necessary changes in their personal life situation in order to implement a foreign set-up in a legal and legally secure manner. Others do not have the means to build up sufficient substance abroad. The consequence is always the same: from the point of view of the tax authorities, they are operating an illegal intermediate company.

By the way: Beyond the foundation phase, a trust director and a virtual office are never enough as substance. A managing director must be employed by the company. The managing director must not be a tax consultant, lawyer or similar service provider - in such a constellation he would always be interpreted as a vicarious agent.

A Regus or virtual office setup is also sufficient as a substance for the start-up phase at most. After that, you have to have your own business premises with a rental contract, etc.

Moreover- also with regard to OECD BEPS- sufficient substance in the company's country of domicile is of crucial importance - at least if the foreign company is a group company that is used to shift profits to tax-favored foreign countries.

Only if the foreign company has sufficient substance is this profit shifting permissible. Otherwise, the parent company is considered a permanent establishment and the seat of taxation.

*The YouPorn example should be a warning to all entrepreneurs who control similar foreign structures and have not yet created enough substance abroad. Build substance or close the company and be sure to get expert advice.*

**Fact 6: The administrative burden for offshore companies increases significantly**

In the past, many offshore companies had a truly paradisiacal situation with regard to accounting and reporting requirements. Very few companies had to keep records or even prepare balance sheets.

More and more offshore countries require an audit certificate. In the meantime, times have changed significantly. The administrative workload of an offshore company is increasing and with it the costs. Company law requirements regarding transparency and documentation are increasing. Other regulations for running a company are also becoming stricter every year.

- In Hong Kong, for example, accounts must now be prepared in the same way as for a European company. In addition, all companies are required to have an auditor's certificate. Even if no taxes have to be paid in Hong Kong, an auditor must certify the company's balance sheet.

- Malta - not an offshore country, but an EU country - is also subject to mandatory certification.
- On the Isle of Man, in Jersey and Guernsey, it is no longer permissible for the client to manage the company's bank account themself (unless they live locally). Rather, a local tax advisor must be appointed as the company's manager, who then manages the company's account.
- Companies in the British Virgin Islands (BVI) are now subject to record keeping and accounting requirements.
- In Ireland - also not an offshore country, but an EU state - non-resident companies (domiciliary companies) are now prohibited, as is the famous Double Irish with a Dutch Sandwich.
- In the UK, bearer shares and trust structures were declared inadmissible in 2015. In addition, as of 2016, companies must report the actual beneficiaries of each company in a new online register.
- Almost all domicile states now prohibit the issuance of bearer shares. And even if you can establish a company with bearer shares, you will not find a bank that will open an account for this company.

These are just a few of many examples that illustrate that running and managing offshore companies is becoming increasingly costly and complicated.

The trend is clearly moving in the direction of higher transparency and increased documentation requirements for corporations.

*It is becoming more unlikely that the bank account of an offshore company is a petty cash fund from which one can simply help oneself. Even well-known tax havens are demanding extensive information about the owners and activities of domestic companies. You should have no illusions in this regard.*

## Fact 7: Opening an account for an offshore company is a complicated and lengthy process

In most cases, the establishment of an offshore company will proceed without any problems. The opening of the account often becomes critical afterwards.

First of all, you will hardly find banks that will open an account for an offshore company without further ado. Banks ask exactly how and for what the account will be used. It is an illusion to think that banks today are still interested in helping someone evade taxes.

Example: HSBC Hong Kong branch

We have heard from quite a few entrepreneurs who flew to Hong Kong to open an account with HSBC for a Hong Kong company. The account was rejected without giving any reason.

Often a business plan must be submitted to the bank. The entrepreneur must also submit a resume.

It is also not uncommon for a background check to be performed, including a simple Google search for your name. If negative or questionable press reports about you appear on the Internet, and possibly articles about possible criminal proceedings, most banks will refuse to open an account.

Some banks charge high fees: For example, we know of a bank in Liechtenstein that retains 6% of the transfer amount as a fee.

Other banks refuse to execute or accept certain wire transfers unless you can provide extensive documentation regarding the transaction.

And always remember: even if you find a bank that opens an account for an offshore company, it will be obliged to report the account movements to the tax authorities as part of the exchange of information.

*Account openings for offshore companies are not easy to achieve. You can often expect 3 months or more for the account to be opened for the company, if an account for an offshore company is opened for you at all. In many cases the bank simply refuses, usually you can only get an account with a referral from an existing client or a locally based intermediary.*

**Fact 8: For whom the use of an offshore company is still harmless today**

Of course, it would be absurd to assume that offshore companies will die out. This is certainly not the case. We refer on this page mainly to the use of offshore companies in the context of tax structuring abuse and tax evasion.

Corporations such as Amazon use large auditing firms for their business model. These are very complex and expensive, so they are out of the question for small and medium-sized companies in this form. Furthermore, large corporations are in a position to conclude tax-favorable individual agreements with governments in certain countries.

Offshore constellations have their legitimate place in tax structuring and wealth planning, and there are a number of scenarios where the use of an offshore company is absolutely legitimate and legal.

Under the following conditions, the use of an offshore company is absolutely harmless:

- You live in a country where there is no CFC regime/offshore tax law (or you move your residence to such a country). If you live in such a country, you will have all the freedom to operate and manage offshore companies. You will also have much less problems with opening an account for the offshore company.

- You operate an actual company of substance in the company's offshore domicile state (i.e. the Bahamas, Isle of Man, etc.), i.e. with business premises, with employees and with a local director.
- You own a corporation or partnership in a country without a CFC regime/external tax law. Said company has enough substance in the country of domicile. This company manages the business of the offshore company.
- You have a trusted person who lives in a country without a CFC regime/offshore tax law. This person is the sole shareholder and director of the offshore company and also has sole account authority. This person may not be a trustee. It is not a vicarious agent. There is no written trust agreement.
- All constructs with offshore companies that are still legal today and have been audited and accepted by tax authorities are, at their core, one of the four scenarios listed above.

Above all, it becomes clear that the establishment of such a structure involves considerable planning and cost effort. This will be worthwhile if a significant financial return can be expected. Also, changes in personal circumstances are to be expected, e.g. a move abroad.

*The use of offshore companies, for example, as instruments of financial and asset planning are still legal and widespread, but only in the context of precisely defined framework conditions that are unobjectionable under tax law. Setting up such a constellation is time-consuming and costly and may mean lasting changes in personal circumstances.*

## Fact 9: There are legal and equally tax-efficient onshore alternatives to offshore companies

Why go far when the good things are so close? It doesn't always have to be the Caribbean if you want to establish a tax-optimized company structure.

Malta (St Julians & Spinola Bay). Your new residence and company headquarters?

There are a number of constellations in Europe and the USA that can be used to realize major tax benefits without risking illegality or having to hide from the tax authorities.

We will briefly address four designs here:

- **Design 1: Move to Malta with Malta company:** You move to Malta and establish a Malta company with a foreign holding company. Malta is the smallest EU state and attracts with numerous tax advantages. A Maltese limited company effectively pays 5% corporate tax. As a foreigner living in Malta, all foreign income is tax free.

- **Design 2: No move abroad. Company in Malta or Ireland with substance:** If you cannot or do not want to relocate, you can still incorporate a company in Malta or Ireland and benefit from the low corporate tax rates (Malta: 5%, Ireland: 12.5%). However, you will then have to build up substance in the company's country of domicile after incorporation: Staff, management and business premises. The substance is very important, otherwise you will face the same problem as the YouPorn founders mentioned above.

- **Design 3:No move abroad.US Inc. with profit transfer agreementanda Scottish LP & Malta Holding with substance: This is a** continuation of the above-mentioned structure 2. However, a US company (Inc.) with a US account is first established (the USA does not participate in the automatic exchange of information according to OECD CRS). This company concludes a profit transfer agreement with a Scottish limitedpartnership(LP). If correctly structured, only 10% of the profits have to be taxed in the US company (with $500,000 profit, $7,500 tax would be due in the US). The rest flows tax-free to the LP. Both the LP and the Inc. are managed by a company in Malta with substance.

- **Design 4: No move abroad.** For example, you participate in a Malta Ltd. through your holding company located in your country of residence. The majority owner and director of this Ltd. resides in Malta and has a long-term residence permit there. The Ltd. has an office and employees in Malta. Possible profit shares of the company are taxed normally in the country of residence via the holding company.

In addition to the immediate considerations regarding substance, the implications of the OECDBEPS project must also be taken into account in all designs. This is particularly important if, for example, infrastructure, including warehouses, is to continue to exist in Germany, France or Austria.

From a tax point of view, it is now problematic if the profit is generated in a tax-favorable foreign country (e.g. Malta), but all logistics services are provided in Germany or Austria, for example. Here, the tax authorities can construct a permanent establishment in Germany or Austria, whereby the profit would not be taxable in Malta, but at least partially also in Germany/Austria.

In principle, always assume that a move to a tax-favorable foreign country has the greatest leverage for you and is associated with the fewest risks. All other arrangements require the creation of substance in the country of domicile of the foreign company, which can be extensive in the long run.

Any entrepreneur who can generate substantial income through a foreign entity should seriously consider moving abroad.

*For EU citizens, it is often more advantageous to use existing EU structuring options than to use a company in one of the typical offshore countries. On the one hand, one is "closer to home" and on the other hand, there are advantages over third countries due to EU-wide regulations (e.g. the EU Parent-Subsidiary Directive).*

**Contact:**

For company formations worldwide, as well as citizenship programs for your second citizenship or but also for diplomatic positions, readers have recommended us the following provider, who can quickly and reliably deliver the said products and has offices in Singapore, Hong Kong and Thailand. He guarantees absolute discretion and protection of your privacy and with 30 years of experience is not a one-hit wonder in this business. In addition, he can provide countless references and is also German-speaking:

www.camel-management.com

info@camel-management.com

**Finally, I did not want to deprive you of a report from BörseOnline magazine dated 15.10.2020:**

Attention, tax authorities! New pitfalls for investors and savers - what you need to know - Hunt for tax evaders

The "FinCEN files" currently show how dirty capital is shifted back and forth around the world. But even blameless investors with foreign accounts are now increasingly coming under the scrutiny of the financial authorities. The Financial Crimes Enforcement Network is making headlines around the world. The research, published under the abbreviated name FinCEN-Files, reveals a data leak by the U.S. Treasury Department. It shows how banks, despite supposedly strict regulations, conducted business with questionable customers worldwide between 2000 and 2017. And this despite the fact that the transactions were suspected of money laundering.

The total volume of "criminal transfers" was $2.1 trillion. The revelation increases the pressure on the international community to soon create more transparency in international money transfers. The downside: even blameless investors with accounts and custody accounts abroad are now coming under greater scrutiny by the financial authorities. The gateway to this is the automatic exchange of information (AEOI), which is intended to "combat cross-border tax evasion" and thus make black money investments impossible. The information transmitted in this way currently enables 110 countries to evaluate the foreign accounts of their citizens. Their national tax authorities report data on all assets of non-resident taxpayers held in bank accounts, securities and life insurance deposits to the tax authorities of the respective home countries on a regular basis. The information is collected from the financial institutions.

These are required to automatically transmit the personal master data of their customers residing abroad to the relevant national financial administration - including the name, address, date of birth, tax identification and account numbers of the respective investor. More and more sensitive data is flowing. In addition, financial service providers must also forward year-end account balances, interest and dividend income, and proceeds from sales transactions involving stocks, bonds, funds and other securities. The German tax authorities receive this data indirectly not only from credit institutions, but also from custodians, foundations, trusts abroad and insurance companies. The latter must also report income from surrenderable life and annuity insurance policies as well as cash or surrender values. These data streams are continuously swelling: According to an evaluation by the OECD, last year the tax authorities of these countries gained insight into 84 million financial accounts that their "residents" had set up abroad - and thus into assets of ten trillion euros. This is almost double the figure for 2018, when information on "only" 47 million financial accounts with total assets of five trillion euros was exchanged under AEOI. Germany alone provided the partner countries with 25 million data records.

Only the Corona crisis can slow down the gigantic data collection somewhat. Due to the pandemic, the AEOI participating countries have agreed at short notice to postpone the regular reporting deadline at the end of the third quarter of this year to December 31, 2020. The previous year's account data will therefore reach the national tax administrations three months later than usual. The responsible authority in Germany is the Federal Central Tax Office (BZSt) in Bonn. This is where it was reported on September 30 of last year that private investors and companies liable to tax in Germany had earned at least 236 billion euros in capital income from their foreign assets in 2018. The actual income is much higher still: AIA reports from relevant countries such as the USA are still pending for 2019.

Sophisticated reporting system: The information held by the BZSt is forwarded to the tax administrations of the federal states. The local tax offices then compare it with the tax files. If the analysis shows that no information on the identified foreign accounts has been provided in the tax returns, the bank customers concerned receive a letter from the tax office - accompanied by a discreet request to quickly declare untaxed investment income or to submit a missing tax return for the year in question as soon as possible. A sophisticated reporting system that could soon expose many more dishonest taxpayers in this country. For by no means all those with unlimited tax liability in Germany have so far disclosed themselves to the tax authorities. "Numerous investors have cleared their black foreign accounts by 2015 and believe that they can get away scot-free in this way," reports Rosenheim tax consultant Anton Götzenberger from his professional practice. "Or they trust that the tax authorities will not be able to evaluate the data transmitted under AEOI." Others hope that only the "big fish" will be picked out and do not count themselves among them. Disastrous legal errors "This misconception could yet be the undoing of many investors," warns Götzenberger, who specializes in the legalization of untaxed foreign assets. Currently, the Munich tax office, for example, is sending letters to German bank clients who have been hit by the Capital Account Reporting Act in Austria. Investors affected in a similar way throughout Germany are also likely to receive unpleasant mail from the tax authorities soon. They can then only argue that a crime discovery has not yet occurred with such a letter. "A conviction for tax evasion solely from the control material can generally not be justified," explains Götzenberger. While German tax offices currently hardly record any voluntary disclosures regarding black money accounts abroad, their number could thus increase again.

New traps for voluntary disclosures: And for another reason: Turkey will report data for the first time at the end of the year as part of the AEOI. This indirectly affects 2.8 million German citizens of Turkish origin, many of whom still maintain bank accounts in their old home country. Corresponding investment income may often not have been declared in German tax returns to date. "In this context, a not inconsiderable number of voluntary declarations can be expected," says Cologne-based lawyer Philipp Külz. In this context, it should be noted: Although the AEI data from Turkey only concern the year 2019, this information generally allows conclusions to be drawn about account balances and income from previous years.

In case of doubt, the German tax office may estimate income in earlier assessment years. Depending on the individual case, capital gains must be fully disclosed for all assessment years retroactively back to 2008. Anyone who only makes disclosures for the 2018 and 2019 reporting years is not making an effective voluntary disclosure. "In order to obtain immunity from prosecution in this way, even subsequently assessed taxes and interest on evasion must be paid in full," explains Munich lawyer Alexandra Kindshofer, who specializes in criminal tax law. In addition, the framework conditions for a voluntary declaration have become increasingly complex in the course of several legal reforms. In the process, repentant tax evaders must observe additional legal deadlines: The criminal statute of limitations is five years, in particularly serious cases it is ten - and the tax assessment statute of limitations can even run for up to 13 years. Critics of the exchange of information, such as the Tax Justice Network, complain that, with few exceptions, no economically poor countries are involved in the AEOI: Wealthy individuals from rich countries could still hide their money without risk by using subsidiaries of their house banks in corresponding offshore areas.

In order to track down black money owners, the German government also wants to speed up the fight against money laundering offenses with the help of a Fiancial Intelligence Unit (FIU). The investigative unit, which is based at customs, collects and investigates conspicuous financial transactions. According to its latest annual report, a total of 114,914 suspicious activity reports were received in 2019. That's an increase of about 50 percent compared to 2018, it said, adding that the annual volume of reports in Germany has increased almost twelvefold since 2009. The FIU attributes the steep increase to the continuous sensitization of reporting offices required under the Money Laundering Act and the progressive automation at major credit institutions. However, around 98 percent of all reports still came from the financial sector. Financial institutions reported 35,000 more suspicious transactions for last year than in 2018. Organizers and brokers of games of chance were primarily responsible for the increase in the non-financial sector. Around 50 percent more reports were also received from the goods traders sector, particularly gold stores, for the past year. Susceptible real estate sector: In addition, the number of suspicious activity reports from real estate agents increased. Investigators have a lot of work to do here: A large part of the untaxed capital of 100 billion euros laundered in this country each year flows into concrete gold.

According to estimates by the anti-corruption association Transparency International, 15 to 30 percent of all money from criminal activities worldwide is invested in real estate. The FIU also recorded a slight increase in reports on cryptocurrencies, with 760 transactions - albeit at a low level overall. In particular, the forwarding of money to trading platforms abroad to exchange the money for cryptocurrencies with subsequent onward transfer typically fulfills the criminal offense of money laundering. "Also, every new money laundering suspicious activity report, due to the expanded group of persons obliged to report, is another reason for a voluntary disclosure," explains tax expert Götzenberger. However, each individual case must be examined to see whether there is already an exclusion for its effectiveness. As effective as the FIU's work is in theory - in practice there are numerous problems: When the authority was launched in 2017, tens of thousands of suspicious activity reports from financial institutions, notaries, brokers and other business entities subject to reporting requirements piled up there. They were often processed by the FIU with delays and errors, criticize the subordinate state criminal investigation offices and public prosecutors. For example, information on suspicious transfers often arrived too late.

An inglorious climax: Since July of this year, the Osnabrück public prosecutor's office has been investigating several FIU officers on suspicion of obstruction of justice. They are alleged to have failed to forward suspicious money laundering reports in eight cases between mid-2018 and early 2020, or failed to do so in a timely manner. As a result, 1.7 million euros are said to have flowed into African countries via accounts at three German banks. "Legislators must decisively drive forward the digitalization and professionalization of money laundering prevention," warns Christian Tsambikakis, Chairman of the Board of the German Association of Money Laundering Officers (BVGB). "Only in this way can the important function of money laundering officers in companies and organizations be strengthened and money laundering sustainably curbed." He said there is still a fear "that an enormously large number of questionable transactions will go unnoticed by the authorities." Tsambikakis also calls on all parties to pull together for this reason: "Germany must not remain a Dorado of money laundering." Critics also complain that the Ban, as money laundering supervisor, does not take decisive action in cases of suspicion - a prominent example being the Wirecard Bank case. They also continue to see enforcement deficits among notaries, real estate agents and auditors who are required to report. The transparency register for companies introduced in 2017 also contains loopholes in the reporting requirements. This limits the quality of the data on actual beneficial owners in companies. Interested parties also complain about the high hurdles to accessing the transparency register: The prerequisite is online registration, for which a copy of identification must be submitted in addition to name, date of birth and address. In addition, there is a fee of 4.50 euros for each document retrieval. The issue of black money will continue to occupy investigators in the future: The loss of income due to short-time work and unemployment as a result of Corona is driving more people into undeclared work in this country, the University of Linz has determined in a study. Their share of the German gross national product will rise from nine to eleven percent this year. That would be an increase of 32 billion euros over the previous year to 348 billion euros.

Under pressure from the European Union, Germany must intensify the fight against money laundering. The legislative changes that have already been implemented and those that are planned are also important for investors: In 2017, the Financial Intelligence Unit (FIU) was separated from the Federal Criminal Police Office (BKA) and the state criminal police offices and located at Customs. Since then, FIU officials have been collecting and evaluating all suspicious money laundering reports from financial institutions, car dealerships and other reporting entities. In this way, the state criminal investigation offices and financial investigation groups of customs and police should only receive "valuable reports" - and be able to pursue suspicious payments more efficiently.

Expanded reporting obligations The 2019 Money Laundering Act reform has redefined and expanded the group of professionals from the financial and non-financial sectors who are required to report. More professional groups are required to report suspected money laundering as of this year. In the real estate sector, the tightening affects brokers and notaries. They must disclose not only the brokerage of sales contracts, but also of rental contracts if the monthly rent is higher than 10,000 euros. For precious metal dealers, the reporting threshold for cash transactions involving bars and coins dropped from 10,000 to 2,000 euros. Elimination of the "predicate offense catalog" In the future, the newly formulated offense catalog is to include all criminal offenses as predicate offenses to money laundering. Theft, embezzlement, robbery, fraud and embezzlement were previously only considered predicate offenses to money laundering if they were committed commercially or by gangs. This proof was often difficult for law enforcement. With the broader scope of application, convicted criminals could soon be convicted of money laundering more frequently than before.

The range of penalties for money laundering will continue to provide for a prison sentence of up to five years or a fine. In particularly serious cases, the penalty will continue to range from six months to ten years' imprisonment. A new feature is that reporting professionals convicted of money laundering will in future face a minimum penalty of three months' imprisonment. Investigators' powers Telecommunications surveillance and online searches will continue to be permissible only in cases of suspected serious money laundering. Court jurisdiction In the future, the white-collar criminal chambers of the regional courts will have jurisdiction for money laundering proceedings if special knowledge is required.

This year, Turkey is participating for the first time in the automatic exchange of information (AEOI) to combat cross-border "tax evasion". It reports data on persons who are resident in Germany and have accounts and custody accounts in Turkey. Nationality is not a factor. Turkish banks and insurance companies are obliged to transmit this information to the central authority responsible in Turkey. This authority forwards the data to the German Federal Central Tax Office as of December 31. If Turkish income is not declared in the 2019 German tax return, there is a risk of criminal tax proceedings.

MALTA: Part of Malta's business model is to issue passports to EU foreigners on request if they buy a significant amount of real estate or Maltese government bonds there. The "golden visa practice" is notorious: Wealthy non-EU citizens are granted citizenship in exchange for investments worth millions. This allows them to move freely and do business in EU countries without taking up residence on the Mediterranean island. The EU has so far urged the Maltese government in vain to take action against financial crime. Nevertheless, Malta has been participating in AEOI since 2016, probably also as a fiscal fig leaf.

AUSTRIA: Former refuge: Until 2017, the Alpine republic was one of the last refuges for black money from Germany, because banking secrecy has constitutional status there. Since 2018, account and deposit balances of more than one million U.S. dollars have been transferred to the German tax authorities under the AEOI. The highest AEOI reporting level came into force in 2019. Assets below one million U.S. dollars are now also covered. German bank customers who cleared out their accounts and custody accounts in Austria between March 2015 and December 2016, withdrawing more than 50,000 euros in cash, must expect data to be disclosed due to the "Capital Transaction Reporting Act."

LUXEMBOURG: Once a bastion, the Grand Duchy has been participating in the AIA since 2016. Before that, its strict banking secrecy made it a popular financial center for black money holders. The focus has since shifted from private investors to corporate clients. Generous financial regulation and corporate tax benefits are expected to attract online merchants and payment service providers in particular. Paypal, Amazon Pay and Rakuten have had their EU headquarters in Luxembourg for some time, and Airbnb was also granted a license to process all EU payments here at the end of 2019. More than 60 financial institutions have relocated to the Grand Duchy because of the Brexit.

SWITZERLAND: The Swiss Confederation is full of tricks: As early as 2014, Swiss financial institutions had asked German clients to come clean to the German tax authorities about untaxed assets in accounts and custody accounts. Nevertheless, in 2019, for example in Bavaria, 48 investors still filed a voluntary declaration due to untaxed capital investments in Switzerland. Since 2017, the Swiss have been transmitting data under the AEOI. A quarter of cross-border assets are managed in Switzerland.

# TOTAL ANONYMITY

**Privacy**

Very few of the readers know that they themselves and only they are responsible for how much information and data is collected, managed and evaluated about them. Most of the time, they themselves unwittingly disclose this data and information and thus put themselves on the line. This begins with the pointless filling out of bait offers, sweepstakes, contests or similar nonsense.

NEVER fill out such a form or take part in such things! Most of the time, these bait offers and promises of profits are used to obtain your personal data and habits in order to use them against you, for example in purchase offers. Often, they are sold on to corresponding companies, which then harass you with mail, phone calls and other contact attempts. Never take part in surveys that are sent to you by phone or mail. NEVER reply to e-mails from senders you do not know and delete them. If you have already made the mistake of returning these things with your information filled in and are now being flooded with advertisements, calls and spam, change your postal address and have the letter carrier return all unsolicited mail with the note "unknown moved" or delete your email address. You will see that you will soon have peace in your box again. And always remember that the first data protection must be with yourself! As a matter of principle, only pass on your personal data to third parties if it is unavoidable.

For orders via the Internet or for information that you request via the Internet, always set up a separate e-mail address that you create anonymously with a provider and use exclusively for orders and inquiries. Keep these mails separate from private mails and messages and NEVER mix them. For your orders, set up an anonymous e-mail account such as: bestellungen@g-mail.com use this account exclusively for your online orders and inquiries to companies and providers.

Try to pay your orders cash by bank transfer or order through an acquaintance, relative or friend or through your own (bogus) company, this way you can keep yourself out of any customer file. If you request information or prices or offers over the Internet, NEVER give your real phone number, NEVER use your own address, they will send you the information by e-mail anyway, so why give this data? Give an e-mail address that they open under a pseudonym and make yourself "Hans Meier"! These are the first steps that will make you disappear from all files or better not appear there at all or only appear with a pseudonym. NEVER answer to so-called "Nachhaker", these are mails which you usually get after a flight, hotel stay, an order, a service or similar, in order to determine whether you were satisfied with the service, the product or the service and the consultation. In each of these letters you confirm firstly that you were also the recipient of the service and secondly you reveal your habits and behavior pattern. This does not have to be the case. Therefore: Simply DELETE!

The first basic rule now gained here is:

**NEVER DISCLOSE YOUR PERSONAL DATA TO THIRD PARTIES, UNLESS THIS IS UNAVOIDABLE AND URGENTLY REQUIRED!**

The same applies, of course, to ALL discount cards, mileage cards, membership cards, payback cards and other nonsense that will only unnecessarily inflate your wallet with a myriad of cards. Basically, the rule here is that NOBODY is giving you a single penny! This "gift" has already been calculated into the price of the normally sold products. In other words your "gift" you have already paid without realizing it.

An old furniture salesman once said to this, "Discount, my friend, let me tell you, is always added on beforehand."

When traveling by air, you usually get every 10th-15th flight in the same class for free, depending on the airline. For frequent flyers this is quite interesting also because of the upgrades, for normal vacationers who fly once a year on vacation, however, absolutely uninteresting. Therefore, consider carefully which membership cards make sense for you at all and whether you really need them. One thing is clear, these cards have only one goal: to store your consumption habits. With every purchase, flight or hotel visit, your data can be exploited. They can create a unique movement and habit profile of you at any time! The same applies to credit cards. They know exactly when and where you refueled and how much you refueled, when you had dinner with how many people in a restaurant or hotelwhat you ate, when and where you flew at what time with whom, when you were at a bar, etc. Think carefully if you want this and if the one free flight or free drink in the hotel is worth this to you and if you want to trade your data for this gift?! Only everyone can answer this for themselves. Personally, I prefer to do without all gifts and stay out of the databases of these data snoopers.

**Residence**

You should also always keep your residence as protected as possible. Of course, you are an honest citizen and have nothing to hide, but you should still protect your home and living space. All VIPs and celebrities do the same!

It is best to always have two addresses. One for your mail and other data stuff and the other where you are actually located. For some, especially those seeking protection, it is also advisable to immediately deregister your residence for a variety of reasons. Then look for a domicile in the neighboring foreign country or however a country, which has best NO obligation to register. These countries include e.g. Great Britain, Paraguay, Panama and many other states.

It is a great advantage to be able to live in one place without having to fill out a registration form with any government agency or office. For example, if you make London your primary residence, no one will bother you there unless you do something illegal. Have your mail and other things sent to a so-called maildrop (P.O. Box address), which you can rent from various providers worldwide.

You can also find someone who, for a small amount, is willing to receive your mail at their address and open and scan it for you if you wish, or forward it to an address. That way, once you unsubscribe, no one will know where you are currently located. If you have to enter an address when deregistering, enter a fictitious address, ideally simply fish one out of the Internet such as an address where a hotel is located.

If you plan to go to London for real, then sign out to Italy to Via do Lores in Rome (Look in a Rome hotel directory and pick a larger hotel in a busy square and use that address for your sign out, of course just name the street and city not the hotel).

Never fly directly to your final destination, but always take a detour. Fly to Italy first, for example, if you want to go to London or Paris. Never take an open jaw flight, but buy the tickets individually. First you buy the flight to Italy and in Italy you buy a new ticket to London or wherever you want to go. Make it as difficult as possible for any pursuers. Shake off everything and as much as possible, because you want to have your peace at your new domicile.

If you need to stay in hotels on your trip, always try to book this through other people. By the way, there are also concierge services for this purpose, which we will gladly name for you. If you do not succeed in this, or in case of acute need for protection, take a prostitute and rent a room in the hotel with her papers. Laugh at a Thai or Filipino woman who accompanies you for quite some time with her papers, but make sure that the person has legal visas and residence permits for the country you are staying in, otherwise you will get into a problem faster than you would like.

You can also stay where you want in Thailand or the Philippines as long as you have a visa. Live with your Thai girlfriend and no one cares about your address. Make sure you always have a valid visa and then to renew it, leave again and enter the same day or the next day, no one cares about you.

Cover your tracks and then travel overland from Thailand to Vietnam or Cambodia or Laos to spend some time there and no one knows where you are. Bus tickets and train tickets are not registered anywhere in these countries. Then fly back to Europe from Vietnam instead of Thailand where you entered. This will make it very difficult for any tracers to track where you are and where you have traveled on to.

**Insurance**

In order to live as inconspicuously as possible, make sure that you completely disappear from the files of the tax office, insurance companies, pension funds or social security, etc.! Of course, you can only achieve this by deregistering and moving away from your previous place of residence and country. Pay your own medical expenses and insure yourself for major damages only abroad. Deregister and do not join such insurance and social systems anywhere in your new residence. Set aside sufficient financial reserves for emergencies and insure yourself only against accidents and unforeseen hospitalizations and operations with a so-called expat insurance. Suitable for this are for example:

www.bupa-international.com
www.expatriategroup.com

The same goes for your car. Try to get along without a car. If you have enough financial means, then you can rent a car for appropriate purposes or rent a limousine complete with a chauffeur for special occasions. Such service is available almost in every big city. In urgent cases, you can also find it in all five star hotels or airports. Otherwise, if there is no other way at all, try to rent your car from an acquaintance or register one through them.

So avoid all registers like tax office, social security, pension insurance, health insurance, car registration, car tax, car registration and car insurance, all discount and payback cards, association and club membership, etc., and all credit cards (pay cash!).

As a matter of principle, always try to stay out of ALL registers whenever you can. Never leave a so-called "paper trail", i.e. a rat's tail of documents, invoices or memberships, etc., from which one can see exactly where you are at the moment, which habits you have and where you had been before. Please note that in today's world, data exchange between countries can take place in a matter of seconds.

**Banking**

When moving abroad, close your previous accounts completely! If you are not able to move abroad, try to use your previous account only for smaller daily transactions.

For all other business you set up an account abroad. For this purpose, you can take any European state to open an account, since there is no longer a banking secrecy anywhere anyway. So it doesn't matter where you have your account. We are talking about a normal checking account and not an account through which you should handle large sums or transactions.

Use the current account to obtain only a prepaid credit card and a normal bank card for cash withdrawals.

Try NOT to have an account in the country you live in and if you have to, use it only for small amounts and transactions. Keep in mind all kinds of reporting limits.

As a general rule, try to pay cash as much as possible and do not use a credit card so that you leave as few data trails as possible.

**Stores**

As a matter of principle, conduct your business through so-called offshore centers and try to maintain the greatest possible anonymity while at the same time maintaining the best possible control over the company or business.

Currently, the best and safest offshore areas for this are Dubai, Singapore and Hong Kong.

As a matter of principle, never conduct your business in the country where you live, but always relocate your company headquarters outside your center of life. Simply set up an English Limited for your business or for each individual activity cheaply and anonymously. You can do this easily online with the following provider:

www.companiesmadesimple.com

If this is also too much for you, then simply resort to the following solution:

Find a friend. Ideally, this friend should live in a remote area such as Africa or Brazil (he can also be from the favelas or slums). Enter his name and address as a director. The English Companies Registry does not generally check entries of directors or shareholders of a company and you can enter whatever you want! This is completely anonymous for you, it is recorded in the commercial register and the company is immediately usable.

In just one day you have founded your "Money Power Ltd." with director Hugo Gonzales from Brazil and this for a measly 30 Britten pounds! It might be more difficult to open an account for this company. If you know Hugo Gonzales personally, he may sign a general power of attorney for you, which you can then use to open an account. It will be even better if Hugo Gonzales opens the account with his Brazilian passport, but then hands over all internet banking access to you, so he cannot access your account himself. Surely you can knit this idea further for your own purposes. The basis for this has been supplied to you.

**Maildrop**

A maildrop is simply a mailbox address that you can rent from professional providers like Regus or other smaller companies. You can set up so-called virtual offices all over the world without ever having taken a single step into that country. As a general rule, if possible, never have mail sent directly to your home. Never give your own home address for contracts, orders or other paperwork. Better use an address provided by an acquaintance or take a mail drop.

Here, of course, it depends on the explosiveness of your business and mail that you need to receive. Depending on what you have in mind, you should keep in mind that, again of course, anonymity stops where you can trace the chain. Most maildrops want to know who you are, demand payment in advance, and want a copy of your ID.

Therefore, always try to find smaller providers that do not require this. However, maybe Hugo Gonzales from Brazil can help you here. He rents the maildrop for you and has the mail sent to him in Brazil first. You then pick it up there personally. If Gonzales lives near the maildrop, he can also pick up the mail for you and send it to you or scan it for you. Again, the best way to do this is to set up a suitable network yourself that meets your needs and is adapted to your situation.

**IMPORTANT: BASICALLY, FOR ALL ANONYMOUS CONSTRUCTS, YOU MUST TRY TO BREAK THE CHAIN AND THE DIRECT LINK TO YOU FROM A CERTAIN POINT.**

**Emails**

As a general rule, always open your e-mail accounts anonymously. Create the account WITHOUT specifying and depositing your personal data. Always use fantasy names and preferably ones that are widely used such as Müller, Meier or Schulze. To be absolutely sure that no direct connection to you can be established, open the e-mail account in an Internet café or via a so-called safer surfer. This prevents you from logging in with your own browser data and protects your IP address and disguises from which network you have just logged in. You will be redirected to a community server abroad and log in to the Internet via this server. This way you are sure that your account has been set up completely anonymously. And this is exactly the method you use to use your account when you want to check or send your mails. NEVER log in to the net from your private browser and server, but always only via the internet café or via a hotel lobby, where you do not have to enter private data and room numbers, or via this Safer Surfer. You can purchase this from:

www.cyberghostvpn.com
www.safervpn.com

And if you really want or need to send e-mails with sensitive data, then I'll tell you how to do this 100% securely without ever running the risk of being caught by a snooping service like the NSA! You say there is no such thing? Yes there is! And it's so primitive that you don't have to have a top training at the secret service to be able to use this so ingenious as well as primitive possibility.

Now you are surely asking yourself the question: How is this supposed to work?

Well, I won't keep you in suspense any longer, the answer is quite simple and primitive that you are about to burst out laughing:

Namely, don't send the email at all, then no one can catch or intercept you!

Yes, you hear right! Do not send your e-mail. Only if you have pressed the "send button" your data will fly into the World Wide Web and can only then be intercepted and fished. But if you don't send anything, then nothing can be intercepted, quite simply. Then of course the question arises: All well and good, but how should my desired partner, whom I wanted to write to, receive the message if I don't send it? Justified question and here is the solution:

You first write the message in your email account normally, as if you were writing a normal email. The only difference now is that when you finish writing your message, you don't send it, but save it in your drafts folder.

Well one should have done certain preliminary work here then.

Set up an anonymous account as already described, then meet with your partner, whom you want to write and give him safely, without anyone knows what it is, the password for your email account! Now you and your partner can log in TOGETHER with the same password.

You've figured out the trick? Now when everything is set up and both parties have the password, you can save your message in the draft folder. You send your partner or the recipient of the mail an SMS with the message " Please retrieve mails".

The recipient now logs into your shared account with your password, goes to the draft folder opens it and reads what you wrote to him. After reading it, he deletes the mail and replies back to you in the same way. Thus you have created a network that no one can penetrate! This works worldwide with countless partners. No one can intercept emails from you, because you don't send any. Nobody hacks into your account, because you NEVER attract attention with this account, because this account NEVER sends anything, but always has only drafts saved, which are then immediately deleted after reading. This method is simple, can be used worldwide, can be used primitively by everyone and is simply ingenious! Try it out, you will be thrilled and will soon be able to sleep well again.

**Internet**

Just as described above, when surfing the Internet, always make sure that you surf anonymously! Surf only in the Internet café or at your home via another surfer, such as Safer Surf offers.

Basically, you are never and NEVER anonymous on the Internet. Constantly, your IP data and surfing data are transmitted in full. So assume that everyone and everything you do on the Internet can be traced back to you. Build in appropriate safeguards against this, as described above with Safer Surf.

Make another protection for your hardware and install a data destroyer on your laptop and PC that is automatically activated if an incorrect password is entered 3 times in a row. This will prevent unauthorized persons from gaining access to your data. In case of burglary or loss of your laptop, you are protected. You can also activate this protection mechanism yourself in case of emergency (e.g. blackmail, coercion or house search), where you are obliged or urged to open your PC or laptop. Just enter a wrong password 3 times and the PC destroys your data by itself and irrevocably overwrites itself again and again. You can then always talk yourself out of it, that unfortunately in the excitement in the corresponding situation you were in, you could no longer reconstruct the password correctly.

Forget basically so-called social networks like Face-Book, Twitter and all the junk! Never register there! Nobody needs to know where you are, in which plane you are flying and in which hotel you are staying, this is all absolute bullshit. Forget about it. This may still be okay for bored teenagers, but even for them the whole information swarm sometimes becomes too much.

The new generation is breeding itself into an absolutely and permanently monitored subject, it doesn't even need a lot of state pressure or help, but they shape their surveillance apparatus completely voluntarily and themselves and without being aware of it.

Also watch out with Google Ads, Paypal and ebay etc. all these accounts can never be cancelled immediately. For data retention reasons, the data collected through these accounts must be kept by the operator for at least 10 years. So better stay away from them if you prefer anonymity.

# GOLD AS AN INVESTMENT

**The value of gold**

Gold has fascinated people since time immemorial. Gold was discovered in the 4th millennium BC and has proven itself through the centuries as the most important means of preserving value. Since ancient times, gold has been considered the symbol of wealth and power. The appeal of the yellow precious metal continues to the present day.

The king of metals and the metal of kings has seen empires rise and fall, withstood wars and financial crises, and to this day is the only money that has been able to maintain its purchasing power worldwide for millennia. At a time when many people feel doubts about the sustainability of our current monetary and banking system, the gold price development has once again attracted a lot of attention.

This precious metal is visually beautiful, relatively rare and not arbitrarily multipliable, in addition, gold has a high value per unit (ounce) and is accepted worldwide. About 2500 to 3500 tons of gold are mined annually, a large part of which is processed for the jewelry industry. Other uses for gold are in industry, minting, investment and health care.

Throughout history, gold was discovered as a means of currency in the form of gold coins. Until 1914, the gold standard was mandatory and the value of money was linked to the price of gold. This was the guarantor of a stable exchange rate system between currencies for almost a century. The most important thing was that the value of money was always measured by gold and never gold by the value of money.

With the failure of the gold standard, not only gold but also the American dollar and the British pound sterling were manipulated into actual currency reserves. Compared to the situation in 1913, when the currency was backed by gold, all currencies have suffered considerable losses in the meantime. The Swiss franc, long traded as the most stable currency in the world, has not even retained a third of the value it had at that time and the U.S. dollar has been on the verge of collapse several times and today has a residual value of not even 10% of the value from the time of the gold standard!

As the so-called book money gained more and more importance in the last 100 years, it was believed that gold was more or less superfluous as a form of investment. The crisis in Mexico and also the crisis in Argentina already showed how the paper money (usually simply printed and issued by the central banks without any cover) of an entire nation can dissolve into nothing overnight. Then, after the Argentine leadership had left behind a 155 billion national debt due to years of mismanagement, it simply resorted to bank closures, account freezes, etc. Nevertheless, the once rich state on La Plata sank into poverty and anarchy.

**ARGENTINA IS EVERYWHERE,**

as you could easily see just recently from the unimaginable dimension of the banking and financial crisis worldwide.

A normal repayment of the debts of the states indebted world-wide up to the ufer-lose is absolutely illusory!

The only alternative left to the states is to print more money, which in turn is uncovered and thus only promotes and intensifies the danger of recession, inflation and even deflation.

Assessing the economic and political situation and forecasting the future are as difficult at the moment as at any time in history. For a long time, however, we have again been experiencing a phase of doubt about fundamental economic and financial principles. This is coupled with the current explosive global political situation. Thus, the investor is confronted with a new and at the same time old challenge to private wealth:

**The safeguarding of one's own assets !!!**

An essential role will be played in this context by an investment that has fallen victim to blind faith in the future and yield dogma over the last twenty years: **THE GOLD.**

## Gold and economic freedom

An almost hysterical hostility against the gold standard unites state interventionists of all kinds.

They seem to feel more clearly and distinctly than even many free market supporters that gold and economic freedom are indivisible, that the gold standard is an attribute of the free market economy, and that the two are mutually dependent and interdependent.

To understand the cause of their hostility, it is first necessary to understand the exact role gold plays in a free society.

Money is the common denominator of all economic transactions. It is the commodity which is used as a medium of exchange and which is accepted by all participants in an exchange society for the payment of their goods. It therefore serves as a measure of market value and for storing value, i.e. saving.

The existence of such a good is the prerequisite for a society based on the division of labor. Without a good that serves as an objective measure of value and is generally accepted as money, people would have to make do with primitive barter. In the other case, they would even be forced to eke out a living on self-sufficient farms and forego the tremendous advantages of the division of labor. If there were no possibility of storing value, i.e. of saving, neither long-term planning nor exchange would be possible. Which means of exchange is acceptable to all economic agents cannot be arbitrarily determined.

First of all, the medium of exchange should be durable.

In a primitive society with only limited wealth, wheat could be sufficiently "durable" to serve as a medium of exchange, since all exchanges would occur only during the harvest or immediately thereafter. There would be no need to store surpluses of value.

But once the store of value becomes significant, as it is in civilized and richer societies, the medium of exchange must be a durable commodity, usually a metal. A metal is generally chosen because it is homogeneous and divisible. Each unit is the same as another, and it can be deformed and alloyed in any quantity.

Gemstones, for example, are neither homogeneous nor arbitrarily divisible.

More importantly, to be suitable as a medium of exchange, the good must be a luxury item. The human need for luxury is unlimited, which is why luxury goods are always in demand and always accepted. Wheat is a luxury good in an undernourished society, but not in an affluent society. Cigarettes would not normally be accepted as money, but after WW2 they were considered a luxury good in Europe. The term luxury good implies scarcity and high value per unit. Because it represents a high value per unit, such a good is easy to transport. For example, one ounce of gold has the same value as half a ton of pig iron.

In the early stages of a developing monetary society, multiple means of exchange are often used, as a whole range of goods can meet the requirements described.

Over time, however, the exchange good that finds the greatest acceptance will displace all others. For the function as a store of value, demand will concentrate on the most accepted good, which in turn will earn it even more acceptance. This development continues until the point where this good becomes the only medium of exchange.

The use of a single medium of exchange has great advantages for the same reasons that a monetary economy is superior to an economy of exchange in kind. It allows exchange on a vastly greater scale. Whether this single medium is gold, silver, shells, cattle, or tobacco varies and depends on the environment and level of development of each society. In fact, all of these commodities have been used as a medium of exchange at different times.

Even in our century, two major commodities, gold and silver, were used as international means of exchange, with gold becoming the dominant one. Gold, which has both artistic and functional uses and is relatively scarce, has always been considered a luxury good. It is durable, easy to transport, homogeneous, divisible and therefore has significant advantages over all other means of exchange.

Before the beginning of World War 1, it was practically the only international exchange standard.

If all goods and services had to be paid for in gold, large payments would be difficult to make, and this in turn would limit to some extent the division of labor and specialization in a society. The logical extension of developing a medium of exchange is therefore to develop a banking system and means of credit (banknotes and deposits) that function as proxies but are redeemable in gold. A free banking system based on gold is able to extend credit and thus create banknotes (currency) and deposits according to the production needs of the economy. Individual gold owners are induced by interest payments to deposit their gold in a bank, upon which they can draw checks.

And since in the rarest of cases all depositors will want to withdraw their gold at the same time, the banker will have to withdraw only a portion of the total

Deposit in gold held in reserve. This allows the banker to lend out more than his actual physical gold deposits (i.e., he holds claims on gold instead of actual gold as collateral for his deposits). But the amounts he can lend are not unlimited. They must be in a sustainable proportion to his reserves and the current state of his investments.

When banks lend money to finance productive and profitable businesses, the loans are repaid quickly and bank credit remains widely available. But when the businesses financed with bank credit are less profitable and slow to be repaid, banks quickly sense that their outstanding loans are too high relative to their gold reserves and they begin to be more cautious about new lending, usually by charging higher interest rates. This limits financing for new ventures and requires existing borrowers to improve their profit situation before they can get loans for further expansion.

Therefore, under the gold standard, a free banking system acts as a guardian of economic stability and balanced growth.

If gold is accepted as a medium of exchange by most or even all nations, an unimpeded free gold standard favors and promotes the worldwide division of labor and international trade. Although the units of exchange (dollar, pound, euro, etc.) vary from country to country, the economies of individual countries function as a single economy, provided all units are defined in gold and there are no impediments to trade and the free movement of capital.

Loans, interest rates and prices then behave similarly in all countries. For example, if banks in one country lend too generously, there is a tendency for interest rates to fall in that country, which causes gold owners to move their gold to banks in other countries where it yields higher interest rates.

This will immediately lead to a shortage of bank reserves in the country with the looser credit conditions, which in turn will lead to tighter credit conditions and a return to competitively higher interest rates.

A completely free banking system and a consistent gold standard have never been realized. But before World War I, the banking system in the United States (and most of the world) was based on gold. Although there was occasional intervention by the state, banking was still mostly free and uncontrolled.

Occasionally, due to too rapid credit expansion, banks had exposed themselves to the lending limits of their gold reserves, whereupon interest rates rose sharply, new credit was not granted, and the economy fell into a sharp but brief re-recession (compared to the depressions of 1920 and 1932, the economic downturns before World War I were mild).

It was the limited gold reserves that stopped an uneven expansion of business activity before it could develop into the kind of disasters that then occurred after the First World War. The periods of correction were brief and the economy quickly regained a sound basis for further expansion. But the healing process was misinterpreted as a disease.

If a shortage of bank reserves causes an economic downturn - the economic interventionists argued - then why not find a way to provide additional reserves to banks so that they can never run short?

If banks could continue to lend money indefinitely, it was argued, there would never again have to be economic downturns. And so the Federal Reserve System was created in 1913.

It consisted of 12 regional Federal Reserve banks, nominally owned by private bankers but actually sponsored, controlled, and supported by the government. Credit created by these banks is in practice (though not legally) backed by the taxing power of the federal government.

Technically, the gold standard remained in place; private individuals were still allowed to own gold and gold was still used as a bank reserve. But now, in addition to gold, credit created by the Federal Reserve banks (paper money reserves) could serve as legal tender to pay off depositors.

When the U.S. economy suffered a mild setback in 1927, the Federal Reserve drew down additional paper money reserves in the hope of forestalling any shortage of bank reserves. Even more disastrous, however, was the Federal Reserve's attempt to help Great Britain, which had lost gold to the United States because the Bank of England refused to let interest rates rise as market conditions should have required (it was politically undesirable). The reasoning of the authorities involved was as follows:

If the Federal Reserve were to pump massive amounts of paper money reserves into the U.S. banking system, interest rates in the United States would fall to levels comparable to those in Great Britain. This would have the effect of stopping the British gold outflows and avoiding the political unpleasantness associated with an interest rate hike.

The "Fed" succeeded: it stopped the gold losses, but at the same time it brought the world economy to the brink of the abyss. The excess money the "Fed" pumped into the economy flowed into the stock market, triggering a fantastic speculative stock boom. Belatedly, the Federal Reserve leadership tried to remove the excess reserves from the market and eventually they succeeded in curbing the boom. But it was too late: by 1929, the speculative imbalances were already so massive that this attempt only accelerated the sharp economic collapse that was already underway. The result was a collapse of the American economy.

Britain fared even worse, and instead of accepting the full consequences of its previous missteps, it abandoned the gold standard altogether in 1931, finally destroying what web of trust remained, leading to a worldwide series of bank failures.

The world economy sank into the Great Depression of the 1930s.

Using the same logic they had used before, the interventionists now argued that the gold standard was primarily responsible for the debacle that had triggered the Great Depression. If the gold standard had not existed, they claimed, England's abandonment of gold payments in 1931 would not have caused bank failures around the world. (The irony was that since 1913 there had been no gold standard in the U.S., but at best what could be called a "mixed gold standard," yet gold was blamed.

But the hostility to the gold standard in any form by a growing number of welfare state advocates was caused by a very different insight - namely, the realization that the gold standard is incompatible with chronic budget deficits (the hallmark of welfare states).

Once you peel away the veil of academic phraseology, you realize that the welfare state is nothing more than a mechanism by which the state confiscates the wealth of the productive members of a society in order to finance numerous welfare projects. Much of the wealth confiscation takes the form of taxes. But the welfare bureaucrats realized that the tax burden had to be limited if they wanted to stay in power. Their alternative was massive government debt, i.e., they must borrow money by issuing government bonds to finance enormous welfare spending.

Under a gold standard, the amount of credit an economy can bear is limited by the real tangible assets of the economy, because every loan is ultimately a claim on a real tangible asset. But government bonds are not backed by real tangible assets, but only by the government's promise to pay from future tax revenues.

Therefore, they cannot be readily absorbed by the financial markets. A large quantity of new government bonds can only be sold to the public at constantly rising interest rates. Therefore, possible government borrowing under a gold standard is very limited. The abolition of the gold standard allowed the advocates of the welfare state to abuse the banking system for unlimited credit expansion. In the form of government bonds, they created paper assets which the banks, following a complicated procedure, accepted as collateral in the same way as real assets, as a substitute, as it were, for what used to be a deposit in gold. The holder of a government bond or a bank deposit based on paper money believes that he has a valid claim on real assets. In reality, however, there are more claims to real values in circulation than there are real values.

The law of supply and demand cannot be repealed. If the supply of money (claims) increases in relation to the supply of real goods in the economy, prices must rise.

inevitably increase. That is, income saved by the productive parts of society loses value in terms of goods. The bottom line of the balance sheet then shows that this loss corresponds exactly to the goods acquired by the government for welfare and other purposes with the money from government bonds financed by credit expansion of the banks.

Without a gold standard, there is no way to save before the expropriation through inflation. There is then no safe

It is no longer a store of value. If that were the case, the government would have to declare its possession illegal, as it actually did in the case of gold.

For example, if everyone decided to exchange all their bank deposits for silver, copper, or some other commodity and then refused to accept checks as payment for goods, bank deposits would lose their purchasing power and government debt would no longer represent a claim on goods. The financial policies of the welfare state require that there be no way for asset owners to protect themselves.

This is the sordid secret behind the demonization of gold by the advocates of the welfare state.

Government debt is simply a mechanism for the "hidden" expropriation of wealth. Gold prevents this insidious process. It protects property rights. Once this is understood, the hostility of welfare state advocates to the gold standard is not difficult to understand.

(Source: The Objectivist, July 1966; German translation by Reinhard Deutsch, edited by Gerhard Grasruck) from the hand of Allen Greenspan, former Chairman of the Federal Reserve Bank of America.

**The gold price development**

Investing financial resources in gold usually follows the desire to make a crisis-proof and inflation-proof investment. In the long term, however, the returns achieved are rather low. The gold price development of the last few years, however, shows an increasing gold price. Thanks to the high demand, the gold price also rose accordingly.

It is never particularly easy to make a reliable forecast about the gold price. However, the current gold price development is obviously strongly linked to the development of the US dollar at the moment. Thus, the gold price has recently shown a high correlation to the EUR/USD currency pair. The gold price is therefore likely to fall as soon as the US dollar strengthens against the euro. This would also break the current upward trend.

Nevertheless, the development of the U.S. dollar plays a rather minor role for gold investors in the EU. This is also due to the fact that an increase in the value of the U.S. dollar could offset losses in the reference gold price. Thus, the gold price development in the EU would be rather positive.

Investors coming from the dollar area can also profit from the current gold price, provided they have a certain risk appetite. The entry opportunities are currently quite interesting in terms of the gold price. Because if the dollar actually rises again, quite high profits are possible for these investors in a short time. However, the risk should always be kept in mind, completely independent of the actual gold price development.

Of course, the price of gold is very much dependent on demand. Times when leaflets and advertising appeals ask for scrap gold to be sent are usually also when there is a particularly high demand for the precious metal. Investors who would like to have the gold they have invested in as real value may have to put up with quite long waiting periods. An increasing need for money in the USA and a possibly resulting inflation would again boost demand and thus also the gold price development. This could even result in an inflation shock. So far, however, the gold price has not been as star k fluctuating as initially feared. However, if the gold price rises sharply again, investors, such as China, should make an immense increase in their gold reserves.

The gold price development still depends on additional factors
. Not only supply and demand determine the price of gold, but also short-term events or speculation. Even emotions are capable of driving the gold price up or down.

Long-term expectations in the gold price development also influence the investment in gold. The oil price is also known for its effects on the gold price. Of course, investors with very large gold reserves, such as central banks, also exert a massive influence on the gold price. For example, market participants with large gold reserves lend gold to depress the price of gold. Or they buy up a lot of gold to increase the gold price. The gold price can be described as volatile due to the changing influences that directly affect supply and demand. For this reason alone, a long-term forecast of the gold price development is not possible even for experts.

Gold is basically a long-term value investment, especially in times of crisis or inflation. As soon as the prices for shares, real estate or funds fall, the price of gold automatically rises. At the same time, money itself loses a lot of its value, as it is produced in large quantities by the central banks in such times. This is necessary to stabilize the economy, but leads to a strong decrease in value. Since gold cannot be artificially produced, it remains valuable and acts as its own currency. Gold buying was also observed by private investors in the wake of the latest crisis. Confidence in governments, banks and paper money led to a drastic increase in gold buying. Currently, everything points to an upward trend.

But even the governments apparently no longer trust their citizens. So the limit for the so-called Tafelgeschäft in Germany (citizens buy gold without naming directly against cash in the store) was lowered drastically.

Until June 2017 the reporting limit was 15,000 euros, until December 2019 it was still 10,000 euros, and from January 01, 2020 the reporting limit according to the Money Laundering Act is now 2,000 euros. In this context, it should also be noted that it is not a good idea to keep gold in a safe deposit box. In addition to the risk of a bank failure, the state also has access to the safe deposit boxes by law as of late.

**Gold price historically in dollars since 1786**

From today's perspective, the historical gold price of 19.49 US dollars in 1786, when the dollar was introduced as a currency, seems almost unreal low. Compared to the all-time high of 2020 with a proud 2023.09 U.S. dollars, the price at 1786 has nominally increased almost a hundredfold.

However, if we take inflation into account, we find that the actual purchasing power of the dollar today is many times lower than it was back then.

The purchasing power of gold, on the other hand, remained comparatively stable, which is why it is still valued today as a store of value and a financial investment. Looking back to 1786, it is particularly interesting to note that the historical gold price in dollars was constant over long periods of time because it was fixed or pegged to the dollar via an exchange ratio set by the U.S. government, which was not lifted until 1971 with the end of the Bretton Woods system.

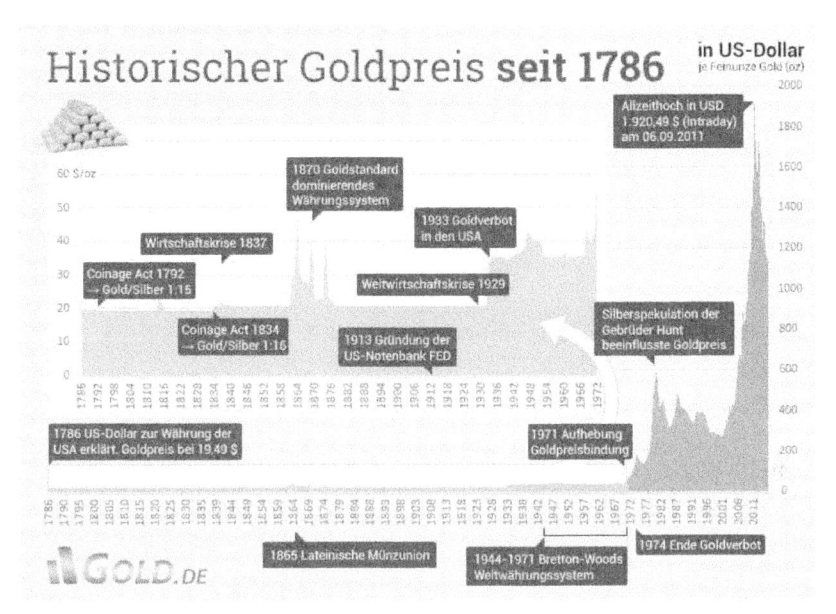

Historical gold price since 1786

**Important key points on the historical development of gold**

Year    Event

1786    US dollar by Congress was declared the currency of the United States

1792    Coinage Act sets gold/silver ratio at 1:15

1812    British-American War

1834    Coinage Act Gold/Silver 1:16

| Year | Event |
|---|---|
| 1837 | Economic crisis and temporary abolition of redeemability of paper money for gold/silver |
| 1844 | Bank of England introduced gold standard (Bank Charter Act 1844) |
| 1861 | American Civil War (War of Secession) |
| 1865 | Latin Coinage Union: monetary union between France, Belgium, Italy and Switzerland. |
| 1870 | Gold standard dominant monetary system as of 1870 |
| 1913 | Foundation of the US Federal Reserve Bank FED |
| 1929 | World economic crisis |
| 1933 | Gold ban in the USA (Executive Order 6102) |
| 1934 | Gold Reserve Act, devaluation USD to $35/oz |
| 1944 | Bretton Woods monetary system (1944-1971) |
| 1971 | Nixon Shock: End of the Bretton Woods World Monetary System |
| 1974 | Gold ban USA lifted |
| 1976 | IMF recommended the removal of the gold peg for currencies |

| Year | Event |
|---|---|
| 1980 | Silver speculation by the Hunt brothers also influenced gold price |

## Gold price development until 2020

- How has gold performed over the long term?
- Where were gold's highs and lows in a given year?

## Development of the gold price by vintages

In addition to the lows and highs, the annual average and performance are also shown.

The gold performance indicates whether the price has risen or fallen and is calculated from the year-end price compared to the year-end price of the previous year.

| Year | High | Low | Average | Close | Performance |
|---|---|---|---|---|---|
| 2019 | 1.552,53 USD | 1.270,54 USD | 1.393,02 USD | 1.515,23 USD | +18,31 % |
| 2018 | 1.358,50 USD | 1.174,16 USD | 1.268,77 USD | 1.280,75 USD | -1,10 % |
| 2017 | 1.349,20 USD | 1.152,15 USD | 1.258,56 USD | 1.295,01 USD | +12,43 % |
| 2016 | 1.370,05 USD | 1.060,85 USD | 1.251,06 USD | 1.151,85 USD | +8,49 % |
| 2015 | 1.302,30 USD | 1.048,30 USD | 1.160,37 USD | 1.061,75 USD | -11,55 % |
| 2014 | 1.390,47 USD | 1.141,54 USD | 1.266,18 USD | 1.200,33 USD | +0,30 % |
| 2013 | 1.693,74 USD | 1.188,10 USD | 1.412,47 USD | 1.196,80 USD | -28,01 % |
| 2012 | 1.793,83 USD | 1.533,49 USD | 1.668,60 USD | 1.662,39 USD | +6,90 % |
| 2011 | 1.908,79 USD | 1.312,83 USD | 1.572,94 USD | 1.555,15 USD | +10,40 % |
| 2010 | 1.421,34 USD | 1.058,00 USD | 1.227,15 USD | 1.408,72 USD | +18,13 % |
| 2009 | 1.212,50 USD | 810,00 USD | 972,36 USD | 1.192,50 USD | +53,28 % |
| 2008 | 1.011,25 USD | 712,50 USD | 871,34 USD | 778,00 USD | -0,80 % |
| 2007 | 841,10 USD | 608,40 USD | 695,22 USD | 784,25 USD | +20,89 % |
| 2006 | 725,00 USD | 524,75 USD | 603,77 USD | 648,75 USD | +29,82 % |
| 2005 | 536,50 USD | 411,10 USD | 444,45 USD | 499,75 USD | +10,36 % |
| 2004 | 454,20 USD | 375,00 USD | 409,17 USD | 452,85 USD | +13,14 % |
| 2003 | 416,25 USD | 319,90 USD | 363,32 USD | 400,25 USD | +26,48 % |
| 2002 | 349,30 USD | 277,75 USD | 309,68 USD | 316,45 USD | +14,51 % |
| 2001 | 293,25 USD | 255,95 USD | 271,08 USD | 276,35 USD | -2,09 % |
| 2000 | 312,70 USD | 263,80 USD | 279,24 USD | 282,25 USD | -2,76 % |
| 1999 | 325,50 USD | 252,80 USD | 278,57 USD | 290,25 USD | +0,85 % |
| 1998 | 313,15 USD | 273,40 USD | 294,12 USD | 287,80 USD | -0,83 % |
| 1997 | 362,15 USD | 283,00 USD | 330,98 USD | 290,20 USD | -21,41 % |

|  | | | | | |
|---|---|---|---|---|---|
| 1996 | 414,80 USD | 367,40 USD | 387,84 USD | 369,25 USD | **-4,59 %** |
| 1995 | 395,55 USD | 372,40 USD | 384,04 USD | 387,00 USD | **+0,98 %** |
| 1994 | 396,25 USD | 369,65 USD | 384,14 USD | 383,25 USD | **-2,17 %** |
| 1993 | 405,60 USD | 326,10 USD | 359,94 USD | 391,75 USD | **+17,68 %** |
| 1992 | 359,60 USD | 330,25 USD | 343,91 USD | 332,90 USD | **-5,75 %** |
| 1991 | 403,00 USD | 344,25 USD | 362,22 USD | 353,20 USD | **-10,07 %** |
| 1990 | 423,75 USD | 345,85 USD | 383,44 USD | 392,75 USD | **-1,47 %** |
| 1989 | 415,80 USD | 355,75 USD | 380,80 USD | 398,60 USD | **-2,84 %** |
| 1988 | 483,90 USD | 395,30 USD | 436,88 USD | 410,25 USD | **-15,26 %** |
| 1987 | 499,75 USD | 390,00 USD | 446,10 USD | 484,10 USD | **+24,53 %** |
| 1986 | 438,10 USD | 326,30 USD | 367,73 USD | 388,75 USD | **+18,96 %** |
| 1985 | 340,90 USD | 284,25 USD | 317,08 USD | 326,80 USD | **+6,00 %** |
| 1984 | 405,85 USD | 307,50 USD | 360,51 USD | 308,30 USD | **-19,38 %** |
| 1983 | 509,25 USD | 374,50 USD | 423,58 USD | 382,40 USD | **-16,31 %** |
| 1982 | 481,00 USD | 296,75 USD | 374,79 USD | 456,90 USD | **+14,94 %** |
| 1981 | 599,25 USD | 391,25 USD | 459,61 USD | 397,50 USD | **-32,60 %** |
| 1980 | 850,00 USD | 481,50 USD | 613,88 USD | 589,75 USD | **+15,19 %** |
| 1979 | 512,00 USD | 216,85 USD | 304,56 USD | 512,00 USD | **+126,55 %** |
| 1978 | 242,75 USD | 160,90 USD | 193,44 USD | 226,00 USD | **+37,01 %** |
| 1977 | 167,95 USD | 129,75 USD | 147,85 USD | 164,95 USD | **+22,41 %** |
| 1976 | 140,35 USD | 103,50 USD | 124,73 USD | 134,75 USD | **-3,92 %** |
| 1975 | 185,25 USD | 128,75 USD | 161,05 USD | 140,25 USD | **-24,80 %** |
| 1974 | 195,25 USD | 116,50 USD | 158,70 USD | 186,50 USD | **+66,15 %** |
| 1973 | 127,00 USD | 63,90 USD | 97,87 USD | 112,25 USD | |

## Supply and demand

Not only supply and demand can determine the gold price, but also short-term events or speculation. The gold price in euros is not least influenced by the development of the exchange rate. Positive or negative sentiment can also drive the gold price up or down: Lost confidence in governments, the banking system and paper money continues to move many investors to buy gold.

In times of high gold prices, there are also more and more private investors who want to sell their gold. Here, too, investors as well as owners of gold jewelry could sometimes profit significantly from the gold price development of the last decades.

## Gold price trend of coins

Investment coins replicate the current development of the gold price quite closely, apart from a small premium.

## A gold price of $65,000?

But what would be the actual price of physical gold without the dampening influence of the fractional and borderless paper gold market. How can we even approach the calculation of a range of such physical gold prices?

Throughout history, gold has been the ultimate money and the ultimate store of value. Until 1971, physical gold backed the international monetary system. Throughout monetary history and into the second half of the 20th century, gold played a crucial role in backing paper currencies and backing monetary debt. It is therefore still appropriate to analyze the value of gold in relation to the value of currencies and the value of outstanding debt.

Throughout history, approximately 190,000 tons of gold have been mined. Almost all of this gold can still be traced in one form or another and is referred to as "above-ground gold." About 90,000 tons of this gold is held in the form of jewelry, 33,000 tons of gold is (allegedly) held by central banks, 40,000 tons is attributed to private gold owners, and the remainder has been used for industrial and other manufacturing purposes.

While 190,000 tons sounds like a lot, at a gold price of USD 1250 per ounce, all gold ever mined in the world is worth less than $8 trillion, and official central bank gold holdings (monetary gold) are estimated at only $1.3 trillion. The U.S. Treasury claims to hold 8133 tons (or 261.5 million troy ounces) in its official gold reserves (a figure, incidentally, that could be much lower, as it has never been independently verified). At the current price of gold, these U.S. Treasury gold reserves are worth just under $320 billion.

Compare these gold valuations with the figures for the total outstanding money supply. The total broad-based U.S. money supply is currently over $18 trillion (using a "continuation M3" measure). For the $18 trillion U.S. money supply to be fully backed by U.S. Treasury gold, a gold price of $68,840 per troy ounce would be required.

Even at 40 percent gold coverage, coverage that has historically been in place for the U.S. money supply in a recent period of U.S. monetary history, this would imply a gold price of $27,500 per ounce.

Excluding the U.S. money supply, the total world money supply is currently over $85 trillion. This $85 trillion global money supply is approximately 11 times the current "valuation" of all gold ever mined.

For the world money supply to be fully covered by the total world gold holdings of central banks [33,000 tons], a gold price of $82,600 per ounce would be required. Even if the world money supply were 100% covered by all the gold ever mined, this would require a gold price of $13,900 per ounce.

According to a recent study by the renowned consulting firm McKinsey, the world's total outstanding debt currently stands at $200 trillion ($58 trillion of which is sovereign debt). For the entire outstanding stock of global debt to be covered by all the gold ever mined, a gold price of $32,700 per ounce would be required. For all sovereign debt to be covered by the official gold reserves of the world's central banks, a gold price of $56,000 per ounce would be required.

Although extrapolations of implied physical gold prices in a world without paper gold market distortions will always be estimates, owning allocated and unencumbered physical gold will be the only way to profit from potential price movements in the physical gold market if and when the fractionally-backed paper gold market ceases to function.

## Physical gold or gold securities?

Gold has always played an important role in the life of man. Even in ancient times, people were enthusiastic about the shiny precious metal. Later, it developed into a globally recognized means of payment. Today, it is used primarily for the production of jewelry and as a financial investment. But those who want to invest in gold today have various options for doing so. While many investors prefer to buy physical gold, others swear by investing in gold securities. Both forms of investment have advantages and disadvantages that should be carefully weighed against each other before making a purchase.

## Buying physical gold: Advantages and disadvantages

The most obvious plus point for an investment in gold is its stable value. For several thousand years, gold has never completely lost its value - on the contrary. If you look at the curve of the price of gold over the last century, you can see that it has multiplied. By buying bars and coins, one owns a physical asset that remains intact even in times of crisis and inflation. Even in the event of a complete collapse of a currency, physical gold remains stable in value. This is mainly due to the fact that man cannot multiply gold at will, as he can do with money. Friends of physical gold are therefore primarily pleased with the stable value and crisis-proof nature of their investment.

Storing precious metals, however, involves a financial outlay, as either a safe for home use must be purchased or an external safe deposit box must be rented. Because the price of gold is quoted in U.S. dollars, the investor can also lose or gain money due to fluctuations in currency rates.

**This is what makes the gold securities**

When trading in paper gold, the investor does not acquire gold, but only securities that are based on the gold price and are traded on the stock exchange. On the one hand, there is the possibility to invest in gold certificates or gold funds. These offer the advantage that the investor can hedge against currency fluctuations. However, this costs the investor fees of two to four percent per year. There is no need to worry about storage and associated costs here. However, the investor bears a higher risk in return. If the issuer goes bankrupt, the certificates issued by him also become worthless and the investor loses his assets.

Unlike gold certificates, gold ETCs are based directly on physical gold. This means that the default risk for the investor is lower. This is because he invests in a certain amount of gold, which he can have delivered to his home if he wishes. The disadvantage of this form of investment is that the investor must also pay annual storage costs for the physical gold, which amount to a certain percentage of the invested sum. If he then wants to have his gold actually sent to him, there are again usually very high delivery charges as well as insurance costs. If the issuer goes bankrupt, the investor also loses his invested capital.

**Conclusion**

Gold securities are particularly suitable for short-term investments, as they are primarily used to speculate on gold price developments without actually moving physical gold. They can be bought and sold more easily than real metal. ETCs offer greater security in this respect, as they are based on physical gold, but its actual delivery involves additional costs.

For this reason, it makes more sense to buy physical gold from the outset if you want to own the precious metal. Only then will you have the pleasure of knowing that gold's stable value is on your side. Investing in physical precious metals is therefore particularly suitable for those who are looking for a long-term investment that is safe against crises and inflation. Nevertheless, it is in principle also suitable for those who would rather speculate on the gold price in the short term.

**The gold price is manipulated**

The gold market is difficult for small investors to understand. Many investors are involved, including the major central banks - and how. Using charts, analysts have discovered that central bankers at the U.S. Fed have manipulated the price of gold for years. In this interview, an analyst explains why the Fed keeps intervening - and what that means for private investors.

**How do central banks influence the price of gold?**

In the past, there have always been conspicuous intraday movements on the gold market - shock-like, short-term price movements to the downside, which at first glance cannot really be explained. In 2001, I examined these movements statistically for the first time. From the anomalies, it can be clearly concluded that someone is deliberately trying to push the price down.

**Sounds a bit like a conspiracy theory?**

But it isn't. The patterns are very striking - and the observations are supported by statements from key central bankers, such as the comment that it is easy to "hold" the gold price.

**Which central banks are steering?**

The impetus for the interventions came from the U.S. central bank, the Federal Reserve (Fed).

**Why would it have an interest in keeping the price of gold artificially low?**

Gold has to do with confidence. The central banks wanted to dampen the population's inflation expectations with their interventions. If the price of the precious metal is low, confidence in paper money is comparatively high, and savers dutifully leave their money in their accounts. A rapid rise in the price of gold, on the other hand, would cause people to fear for their savings because they believe that inflation rates will rise sharply in the future. They would invest their money in real assets instead. A wage-price spiral could be the result and ultimately actually lead to a sharp rise in inflation rates.

**Since when is the price controlled?**

Systematic interventions began on August 5, 1993.

**Why is the price of gold so easily manipulated?**

Gold is predominantly an investment good, not a consumption good. It is stored in large quantities. In recent years, the central banks have dumped many times their annual consumption on the market, a total of around 8,000 tons. The quantity sold or lent alone influences the price. But there is a second, often neglected aspect. Gold loses its attractiveness as an asset if its price does not rise, i.e. if it is depressed by central bank intervention. It becomes less interesting for investors, since it does not yield any current income. For a consumer good, it's the other way around: if its price falls, more will be demanded and consumed. You can check your behavior at the gas station.

**Many Asian central banks, on the other hand, are buying more gold. In times like these, isn't it advisable to keep your gold holdings together?**

What is advisable from the central banks' point of view - and what is not - is difficult for me to say. What is certain, however, is that central bankers have changed their minds about gold more often in the past. Since 2001, they have tended to let the price rise and only dampen it, as happened after the bankruptcy of the U.S. investment bank Lehman Brothers. At the time, the aim was to calm the financial markets. If the gold price had risen even more sharply in this environment, it would have further increased the panic on the stock markets. In the end, however, it has to be said that the number of central banks buying at the moment is very manageable. This also applies to the volumes that are being moved.

**In other words, will the major central banks continue to sell off their holdings in order to keep the price artificially low and calm the markets?**

As I said, they have their opinion on gold in the past changed more often.

**Gold Price Manipulation**

For some, it's a foregone conclusion; for others, it's just a conspiracy theory that doesn't merit further discussion. Are the concerns about government intervention in the gold price trend well-founded?

**Background: The monetary role of gold**

Together with silver, gold was one of the most important means of payment for thousands of years and was the yardstick for value par excellence for long stretches of history. The U.S. dollar, too, owed its legitimacy as the world's reserve currency in the Bretton Woods system of the -Woods-Systempostwar era to the value of one troy ounce of gold until the 1970s.

It was not until Richard Nixon unilaterally announced the convertibility of dollars into gold in the so-called Nixon Shock of 1971. The U.S. president thus initiated today's system of physically unbacked fiat money that can be (and is) multiplied at will. Since fiat money literally created out of thin air no longer has a physical anchor in the form of gold, there remain two ways to assess the value of the dollar:

External value can be expressed in exchange rates against other currencies, and changes in value within the U.S. by the inflation rate. However, according to many critics, both gauges are now unsuitable for measuring real changes in the value of money (more on this below).

**"Loud voice" of gold feared**

Gold can still perform the monetary function. The precious metal does not play a role in payment transactions and is no longer formally used to back currencies. However, the precious metal has retained its monetary character to this day: In addition to foreign currencies such as the dollar, euro and yen, central banks also hold gold as an official part of their foreign currency reserves, in some cases to a considerable extent.

The share of gold in reserves is now between 60 and 75 percent in the USA, Germany, France and Italy. Instead of saying, "One troy ounce of gold is worth $1,000," it is equally possible and correct to turn the valuation yardstick around: "1,000 dollars (or 1,000 euros, yen, etc.) one troy ounce of gold is worth." According to proponents of the theory of gold price manipulation, it is precisely this value-measuring property, the "loud voice of gold" as it were, that constitutes a conclusive motivation for intervention in gold price developments by central banks.

There is little to counter this argument. Rising debt and the bloated balance sheets of governments and their central banks make it obvious that they have an interest in demonetization. The fact that this demonetization is actually taking place can be seen not least from the sharp rise in money supply.

## Government Debt, Central Bank Balance Sheet and Money Supply Using the Example of the U.S.A.

Here is an overview of the development of U.S. government debt, the Federal Reserve's balance sheet, and the M2 money supply in the U.S. since the beginning of the financial crisis starting in 2007. The broader M3 money supply, which in addition to M2 includes balances of more than $100,000 in U.S. accounts, as well as Eurodollars (bank deposits with a maturity of up to six months outside the U.S.), has not been published by the Fed since 2006.

| Year | Govt. Debt Share of GDP in % | Balance sheet of the Fed * | M2 money supply * |
|---|---|---|---|
| 2007 | 64,8 | 890,7 | 7.446,5 |
| 2008 | 76,0 | 2.136,9 | 8.196.3 |
| 2009 | 87,1 | 2.234,1 | 8.454,1 |
| 2010 | 95,2 | 2.420,6 | 8.796.0 |
| 2011 | 99,4 | 2.926,1 | 9.623,0 |
| 2012 | 100,83 | 2.907,3 | 10.484,5 |
| 2013 | 101,17 | 4.032,5 | 10.992,6 |
| 2014 | 102,98 | 4.497,6 | 11.657,1 |
| 2015 | 104,17 | 4.482,3 | 12.322,4 |

* in billions of dollars

**Currency race to the bottom**

If increasing government debt, an inflated central bank balance sheet and a rising money supply were a purely U.S. phenomenon, currencies such as the euro, the yen and the British pound would be steadily appreciating against the U.S. dollar. However, this is not the case, as the UK, Japan and the eurozone are also pursuing an equally aggressive and in some cases even more aggressive policy of demonetization by means of bond purchases, rock-bottom interest rates and, since 2016, in some cases even negative interest rates.

In 2015, public debt in the United Kingdom was 88.6 percent of economic output, in the eurozone 93.5 percent, and in Japan as high as 229 percent. The exchange rates of these countries and currency areas can now be understood more as a gauge of relative weakness than relative strength. This is why there is often talk of a "race to the bottom" between all the major foreign exchange currencies.

**Hidden inflation**

The performance of a currency within a country or currency area can be measured by the inflation rate. On closer examination, however, inflation turns out to be just as imperfect a measure of valuation as exchange rates. Inflation is defined as a general and sustained increase in the level of goods prices.

What is actually measured, however, is the price development of baskets of goods, i.e. selected products and services. The selection and weighting of these products open up a wide range of possibilities for giving the inflation rate the right "look", i.e. for "adjusting" it downward. The fact that adjustments are made in the calculation on an ongoing basis is undisputed. The effect is quantified differently by various critics.

For the U.S. dollar, shadowstatistics.com, for example, estimates that inflation based on 1990 calculations was around 5 percent at the beginning of 2016, while the U.S. Consumer Price Index (continuously adjusted since 1990) gave an inflation rate of 1.4 percent.

So what is left as an accurate gauge of a currency's value?

The answer: the price of gold.

## Gold price manipulation on the COMEX

The COMEX in New York and, by extension, the electronic trading platform GLOBEX are cited as an important crime scene for the assumed gold price manipulation. Futures, i.e. commodity futures contracts on gold, are traded on both trading venues. Physical delivery plays no role in trading, or only a very minor role.

The ratio of traded futures to eligible stocks is typically well below 10 percent, and the ratio to registered stocks is well below 1 percent. The current figures can be viewed on the website of the exchange operator CME Group. The largest participants in gold futures trading are the so-called bullion banks such as JP Morgan, HSBC and the Bank of Nova Scotia.

The U.S. Federal Reserve, it is alleged, is using these bullion banks to depress the price of gold with uncovered short sales. Uncovered short sales are sales of gold that does not exist in real terms. This creates an artificial supply that no longer has anything to do with the real relationship between gold supply and gold demand.

## Evidence of gold price manipulation on COMEX

Evidence for manipulation of the market with gold futures is abundant. The most striking is the atypical way in which large volumes of sales are placed on the market and when.

A seller of futures has a natural interest in hiding a high volume of selling as much as possible so as not to negatively affect the price through oversupply. This concealment works best during the most active trading period and by breaking the sale into many small orders that appear on the market spread out over time and can thus be absorbed more easily.

On the COMEX and GLOBEX, the exact opposite behavior could be observed again and again over the years. Massive orders were placed in the quietest times, which each time resulted in the expected effect of an immediate sharp drop in prices. There is no other reasonable explanation for this otherwise perverse action than an attempt to depress prices.

## Examples of probable gold price manipulation on the COMEX

Concrete examples of such attacks on the gold price in the futures market can be found in many places. A particularly obvious case from January 6, 2014 is described by Paul Craig Roberts, Deputy Treasury Secretary of the USA under Ronald Reagan and certainly no wild conspiracy theorist in his essay: "The Hows and Whys of Gold Price Manipulation".

"After gaining $15 in the Asian and European markets, the price of gold suddenly plummeted by $35 at 10:14 a.m. In less than 60 seconds, 12,000 contracts were traded, representing 10 percent of the total trading volume that day." (?)

"There was no news or event in the market that could have triggered this massive increase in COMEX futures sales." (?) "The 12,000 contracts represent 1.2 million ounces of gold, an amount that exceeds everything in COMEX warehouses for delivery by a factor of three."

Another example of probable gold price manipulation via the GLOBEX trading platform dates from December 18, 2013. In several waves and within an effective trading time of 6 minutes, contracts with a total volume of 37.6 tons were thrown onto the market, pushing the gold price down by more than $50 at times.

**Gold price manipulation through gold lending**

While the suspected manipulation of the futures market involves purely paper trades without delivery, gold lending actually involves the movement of physical precious metal.

Central banks, such as the U.S. Federal Reserve and the Bank of England, hold significant amounts of gold for the central banks of other countries. In the case of gold lending, some of this gold in custody is now "lent" to bullion banks, which then make it available to the physical market in London. Formally, this does not change the ownership claims of the countries using the deposit service. However, the gold claim is no longer fully covered by real precious metal.

At the same time, a supply is created on the physical market that would not exist without the "borrowed" gold. In a very similar way, the major bullion banks also "borrow" gold from customers for whom they store the precious metal. Gold lending is not a new phenomenon. It goes back centuries and was first carried out by goldsmiths who stored gold for customers.

The practice of gold lending is based on the recognition that the probability of delivering larger quantities of gold at the same time is extremely unlikely. Thus, even today, there may be more claims on gold than there actually is gold. However, this ratio of real gold to claims on gold cannot be extended to infinity.

The critical point is reached when physical deliveries can no longer be met. Two important aspects suggest that this critical point is near, namely the strong demand for gold in Asia on the one hand and the retrieval actions of gold from New York and London by a number of states on the other hand.

**Gold repatriation**

The growing mismatch between physically available gold and gold claims at the Federal Reserve and the Bank of England, created by the practice of gold lending, has not gone unnoticed by governments and central banks around the globe. Germany is just one of numerous countries that have started or already completed repatriations, or repossessions. Other countries include Venezuela, Austria and the Netherlands.

In January 2013, the German Bundesbank announced that 300 tons of gold from New York and 374 tons from Paris were to be transferred to Frankfurt. The envisaged repatriation period of seven years at least suggests the suspicion that most of the German gold has also been "lent out", i.e. it only exists on paper within the central banking system and has to be procured anew in a lengthy process. By way of comparison, it took Venezuela five months (August 2011 to January 2012) to repatriate 160 tons of gold.

## Asian demand empties Western gold vaults

While for Western central banks or investors gold ownership in the form of partially uncovered claims was considered unproblematic until a few years ago, physical demand from Asia requires the precious metal immediately. A large part of the gold is required for the production of gold jewelry and gold bars for investment purposes are also demanded in physical form.

This became impressively clear in 2013, when Swiss refiners had to remelt en masse the 400-oz gold bars commonly used in the London trade into the smaller 1-kg gold bars preferred in Asia. Chinese demand alone reached an all-time record of more than 1,100 tons in 2013, and in India demand was hardly lower at 975 tons.

Is the gold coming out of the Bank of England vaults? This much, at least, is indisputable: The Bank of England announced in April 2013 that its stockpiles had fallen by 1,300 tons. The gold was probably not the property of the United Kingdom's central bank, but precious metal held for other countries. The second important source was the holdings of gold ETFs, which recorded outflows totaling more than 1,000 tons in 2013. At the same time, a concentrated attack on the gold price for April 2013 can be assumed with at least some justification.

**Gold price crash in April 2013**

With gold prices above $1,600, investment bank Goldman Sachs issued a new price target of $850 and urged investors to divest their physically backed cash holdings - read: ETF shares. At the start of trading on April 12, contracts with a volume of 400 tons of gold were thrown onto the market on the COMEX, initiating a two-day crash in the gold price of more than 15 percent. Not since 1980 had the gold price plummeted so sharply in such a short period of time.

The crash led to panic selling of ETFs. The largest of the gold funds, the SPDR Gold Trust, held over 1,150 tons of gold on April 12, 2013. By the end of April, holdings had fallen to less than 800 tons. The theory that the gold price was deliberately depressed in April

2013 to meet pending deliveries from Asia will never be proven, but it is certainly plausible.

In any case, the gold price did not fully recover from this shock for a long time. Three years later, in April 2016, the precious metal cost between 1,200 and 1,300 dollars, after the previous low of around 1,050 dollars had been marked in December 2015.

## The extreme levels of the real "inflation-adjusted" gold and silver prices

In economics, a real value refers to any value that has been adjusted for inflation. A nominal value is a value that has not been adjusted for inflation. Inflation here refers to the general increase in the price level.

Many readers will be familiar with inflation adjustments applied to GDP, wages, interest rates, securities yields and, of course, consumer prices and asset prices. The resulting data are usually referred to as "real = inflation-adjusted" data.

Economic data are adjusted for inflation so that data measured over a period of time take into account the rate of inflation over that period and remove the distorting effect that such inflation would have on the comparison of data points over time. Inflation is measured by calculating the rate of change in the prices of a basket of goods and services, such as a Consumer Price Index (CPI) or a Cost of Living Index (COLI).

However, the critical variable in any inflation adjustment is what inflation rate is used and whether one can trust the calculation of that inflation rate and its methodology and the resulting outcomes.

Governments have a vested interest in reporting a low inflation rate so that economies appear healthy and inflation-linked government spending in the form of pensions, Social Security, and inflation-linked debt is minimized.

Central banks have a vested interest in indicating a low inflation rate, as this makes the purchasing power of their fiat currencies look less weak than it actually is. At the same time, negative interest rates are hidden during low interest rate environments.

In the U.S., the most widely used calculation of inflation is the U.S. government's Consumer Price Index (CPI) series, calculated by the U.S. Bureau of Labor Statistics (BLS). These indexes are a fiction, if not an outright lie, as the BLS's motivation is to understate inflation for their political paymasters for the reasons stated above. For this reason, alternative inflation rate providers such as ShadowStats have emerged to counter the government's version of inflation with a more truthful and factual alternative.

For example, the Bureau of Labor Statistics tells you in its latest release, dated January 13, 2021, that annual inflation based on its flagship Consumer Price Index for All Urban Consumers (CPI-U) was only 1.4% for 2020.

Whereas, ShadowStats Alternate CPI (1980 Base) noted in its January 14 daily update that annual average inflation in 2020 was 8.9%.

The difference is massive and striking. And when you add up these differences between the increasingly U.S. government-modified CPI numbers and the earlier 1980 methodology, the differences in inflation rates and inflation adjustments are staggering.

ShadowStats states that its Alternate CPI:

"reflects the CPI as if it had been calculated using the 1980 methodology."

In general, methodological shifts in government reporting have depressed reported inflation. The concept of the CPI is far from being a measure of the cost of living required to maintain a constant standard of living.

ShadowStats also says, "ShadowStats' alternative CPI-U measures are an attempt to adjust reported CPI-U inflation for the effects of methodological changes in recent decades."

In short, ShadowStats says here in an article explaining the Bureau of Labor Statistics' shenanigans:

"that since the early 1980s, the consumer price index has been reshaped to understate inflation relative to general experience."

**Real = inflation-adjusted prices - CPI versus ShadowStats**

Accurate inflation numbers are always important, but arguably even more so in the current global environment of financial repression imposed by central banks and governments through unlimited global quantitative easing, multi-trillion dollar economic stimulus, rapid growth in the global money supply, and low to negative interest rates.

Unlimited money printing and the destruction of fiat currencies ultimately lead to high inflation and possibly hyperinflation, and there should be a set of working alarm bells that signal the onset of these phenomena.

While rising prices in general commodities, raw materials and bitcoin seem to be doing their job correctly as alarm bells signaling higher inflation expectations and a race to the bottom in fiat currency values, central banks have for now managed to eliminate the traditional inflation barometer in the form of a rising gold and silver price in U.S. dollars. At least, that's what they think.

But as with all manipulations and interventions, the central banks and their government schemers, by suppressing the inflation data, have only made the future upward movements in the prices of monetary metals all the more spectacular when the paper gold swindle finally comes to an end. And they have also left all the evidence in the form of real = inflation-adjusted gold and silver prices for everyone to see.

While this is even obvious when using US CPI data as an inflation adjustment, it is much clearer when gold and silver prices are adjusted for inflation using ShadowStats Alternate CPI data, as you will see below using gold and silver price charts from the website GoldChartsRUs. These charts use prices adjusted for historical inflation through December 2020.

At the heart of the inflation-adjusted gold price data series is the legendary spike in the price of gold in U.S. dollars in the late 1970s and into January 1980, a spike that peaked on January 21, 1980, with the price of gold at $850, a level that would become a multi-year high for the nominal price of gold.

Although this is now 41 years ago, this $850 level is critically important as it still appears to be the peak for the real = inflation-adjusted gold price when adjusted for inflation (by all inflation measures).

**CPI Adjustment - Gold**

**The diagrams for this can be found on:**
**www.GoldChartsRUs.com**

The first chart is a long-term chart of the price of gold in U.S. dollars since 1700, adjusted for inflation by the Bureau of Labor Statistics' U.S. Consumer Price Index (CPI-U).

You can see that based on this CPI adjustment, the all-time high for the U.S. dollar gold price was **$3045** per troy ounce in January 1980.

The next chart shows the same data, but magnified from 1950 to December 2020. The key takeaway from these charts is that the U.S. dollar price of gold (which is currently $1830 at the time of writing) is still 66.4% below its all-time high in real terms, adjusted for the consumer price index, even after adjusting for the incorrect and intentionally understated U.S. government inflation statistics.

**CPI Adjustment - Silver**

As for silver, there were two known historical peaks in the U.S. silver price, the first at $49.45 per troy ounce on January 18, 1980 (which was related to the Hunt Brothers trade), and the second just under 10 years ago on April 28, 2011, when the price spiked at $49.20. Although these two peaks were similar in nominal terms, one preceded the other by 31 years, and so the inflation adjustment will be greater for the 1980 peak price than for the 2011 price.

If we look at the long-term chart of the silver price in U.S. dollars since 1700, adjusted for inflation by the Bureau of Labor Statistics' Consumer Price Index (CPI-U), we can see that, similar to gold, the silver price peaked in the early 1980's and that the inflation-adjusted peak of the silver price, using the intentionally attenuated CPI adjustment factor, was an impressive **$140.85,** which would be an incredible 469% above the current silver price of $24.75 (at the time of this writing).

Looking at a more zoomed-in version of this chart starting in 1950, the real peak in 1980 becomes clearer compared to the peak in 2011.

### Shadow statistics- Adjustment- Gold

Moving beyond the manipulated inflation data released by the U.S. Bureau of Labor Statistics, we take a look at gold and silver prices adjusted by ShadowStats' alternative CPI (1980 base).

As a reminder, this alternative CPI from ShadowStats is an estimate of inflation to date, as if it had been calculated using the methods used by the Bureau of Labor Statistics in 1980.

Using this alternative CPI, the real = inflation-adjusted historical prices of gold and silver become exorbitantly high.

The first chart above is a long-term chart of the price of gold in U.S. dollars since 1700, adjusted for inflation using ShadowStats Alternate CPI. The peak of the gold price in January 1980, adjusted for inflation, is **$20,900.24** per troy ounce. Yes, you read that correctly. Nearly $21,000.

In other words, in real terms, the current U.S. gold price of $1830 is massively below gold's all-time high, and 1042% below its real all-time high.

The enlarged version of this chart from 1950 more clearly shows this massive inflation-adjusted peak of nearly $21,000 and also illustrates the Bureau of Labor Statistics' political manipulation to suppress inflation data since 1980 and destroy gold's traditional inflationary price signals.

**Shadow Statistics Adjustment- Silver**

The ShadowStats Alternate CPI adjustment of historical US dollar silver prices is equally impressive. Using the same ShadowStats Alternate CPI (1980 Base) data series to adjust silver for inflation, the true all-time high in silver prices is an incredible **US$966.77,** recorded during the January 1980 high. Yes, that's almost US$1000.

This real inflation-adjusted all-time high is 3800% above the current US dollar silver price.

An enlarged version of ShadowStats' inflation-adjusted silver price series from 1950 to December 2020 is shown above, with the January 1980 inflation-adjusted all-time high of nearly US$1000 per troy ounce.

**Conclusion**

Nominal gold and silver prices in U.S. dollars are currently well below their real (inflation-adjusted) all-time highs. And this is true even if one uses the corrupted, artificial, and politicized CPI data from the U.S. government's Bureau of Labor Statistics. Even those who believe in the official CPI data have to wonder why gold and silver prices have not kept pace with the U.S. government's officially released inflation statistics. How much longer can the charade of the paper gold and silver market be maintained as the U.S. moves toward the destruction of the U.S. dollar with ever-increasing banana republic policies?

**Warning**

**Basically I recommend to every investor who would like to have the gold as a security, exclusively to the purchase of physical gold! Many of these so-called in gold covered papers and investments, are just not covered with enough gold. There are 100,000 x more contracts and gold volumes on the market, than gold for these contracts for delivery exists at all. In addition, should there be a crash, then your papers are also affected and no bank or broker will deliver just one gram of gold to you. Even the Deutsche Bank could not pay out their investments covered in gold to the investors. Therefore it applies to acquire in principle the gold exclusively physically and to store bank-independently!**

**When buying gold, you should pay attention to the following:**

1. Buy only PHYSICAL GOLD! So gold in coins and bars.

2. Never store your gold in a bank, but always bank independent!
3. When buying silver, always make sure that you buy it in a country that does not charge VAT or that you keep it in a duty-free warehouse.
4. Try to split your storage into 2 or 3 different countries.

Very good experience of our customers was reported to us during storage at the following company:

www.bitgold.asia

This company stores precious metals for you in Singapore and Hong Kong. Here you can pay with fiat money as well as anonymously with cryptocurrency. You will receive a notarized certificate of deposit and a photograph of your physically stored precious metals. Here you can get not only gold but also silver or platinum in the form of bars and coins. You can have your precious metals physically delivered to you at any time, or you can have them paid out. In addition, you can also pay anonymously with cryptocurrency here (see also the chapter cryptocurrencies).

## What is special about storing and buying physical gold in Singapore?

Due to its location between India and China - the world's largest consumers of gold - Singapore's port is one of the busiest in the world. The city-state of Singapore is rightly described as one of Asia's most important trading centers. It is located at the southern tip of Malaysia, near the Strait of Malacca, which connects the Indian Ocean with the Pacific Ocean. The island republic is generally known as business-friendly and it has low tax rates, a stable parliamentary democracy and entrenched property rights.

Singapore's crime rate is very low, and its citizens are quite wealthy. Globally, it has the third highest gross domestic product in the world. The Singapore government is a net international creditor. It runs a structural surplus between its revenues and expenditures every year.

For both gold and silver the commission and storage charges are the same as at all other BullionVault locations. You can also trade gold and silver in Singapore around the clock, seven days a week.

# CRYPTOCURRENCIES

## What is Bitcoin?

There are now endless new cryptocurrencies since the first introduction of the Bitcoin cryptocurrency, which I will come back to later. However, I would like to start with the explanation for the first cryptocurrency developed worldwide, Bitcoin. The term Bitcoin is composed of the words "bit" (from English binary digit meaning 0 or 1) and "coin" (English for coin). The concept of the digital currency was described by the author Satoshi Nakamoto in a "white paper". Nakamoto is probably not a real person, rather the name is either a pseudonym or stands for a group of people. The so-called cryptocurrency is intended to enable a monetary system that functions independently of states and banks and is cheaper and faster than previous transactions. The digital currency is traded "peer to peer", i.e. directly between users, without the help of banks. This is made possible by the use of blockchain technology: within the system, all transactions are stored many times and in a decentralized manner.

## How long has Bitcoin been around?

In 2007, someone under the pseudonym Satoshi Nakamoto began working on digital currency. Shortly after the insolvency of the U.S. investment bank Lehman Brothers triggered the global financial crisis in 2008, a nine-page script ("white paper") appeared on the Internet describing the basics of a new, virtual currency: "Bitcoin: A Peer-to-Peer Electronic Cash System".

The founding document described in detail the technical and economic foundations of the currency. In February 2010, the first online Bitcoin exchange opened. The first real-world Bitcoin payment took place in May 2010: A programmer in Florida paid 10,000 Bitcoins for two pizzas (which were thus worth over $170 million in December 2017). In late 2010, the first Bitcoin transaction between two smartphones succeeded. In early February 2011, 1 Bitcoin was worth the same as 1 dollar for the first time. First Bitcoin exchanges outside the US emerged. In September 2012, the Bitcoin Foundation was founded. This aimed to financially support the core team of software developers and continuously improve the Bitcoin network.

**Why all of a sudden this huge interest in Bitcoin?**

For a long time, cryptocurrencies and with them Bitcoins were a topic for computer experts, mathematicians and monetary policy revolutionaries. Libertarian free spirits and opponents of monetary policy determined by central banks saw in the new currencies an opportunity to no longer be dependent on the now ultra-expansive monetary policy of central banks or the budgetary policy of over-indebted states. More or less half-secret organizations also recognized the potential of the new technology to move funds anonymously on the Internet.

But then speculators discovered the price potential of Bitcoin - this trend has accentuated in 2017. At the beginning of the year, the digital currency traded at over U$ 10,000, and towards the end of 2017, the cryptocurrency exceeded the U$ 19,000 mark. Market observers assume that only a low single-digit percentage of the coins is used for payments.

Investors hoard the rest in the hope that prices will continue to rise. As a result, supply remains tight amid rapidly rising demand. At the beginning of December, several options exchanges in the US decided to launch futures contracts on bitcoin. This means that bets can also be made on falling bitcoin prices. This circumstance now makes cryptocurrencies attractive for institutional investors such as hedge funds.

There were already investment products on the Bitcoin, for example tracker certificates in Switzerland. A private bank also offered blockchain asset management. In the wake of the Bitcoin rise, a rapidly growing biotope of cryptocurrencies is developing. By means of issuing new entitlements to cryptocurrencies, so-called Initial Coin Offerings (ICO), the supply is growing daily. But the field of application goes beyond pure payments.

Blockchain technology also enables other secure transactions without an intermediate instance - such as real estate transactions; the role of the notary will thus be taken over by the blockchain. How does Bitcoin differ from "normal" currencies? The biggest difference between cryptocurrencies and traditional currencies is that they are not linked to a country's monetary policy and central banks do not have the exclusive right to issue them.

The number of Bitcoins is capped at 21 million. This is intended to prevent inflation. Central banks, on the other hand, can create money without a cap - as has been shown in recent years - if that is what their monetary policy requires. However, although Bitcoin has set out to make central bank currencies obsolete as cryptocurrencies, Bitcoin, like central bank money, is (ideally) divisible, durable, transportable, difficult to counterfeit and, above all, scarce.

## Besides Bitcoin, there are now plenty of other cryptocurrencies. How do they differ?

As recently as 2011, Bitcoin was the only cryptocurrency. But the convincing concept led to numerous alternative currencies ("alt coins"). There are now over 1300 of them. Bitcoin's main competitor is Ethereum's Ether. Created in 2013 by the then 19-year-old Vitalik Buterin, the technology is also based on the blockchain, but is more powerful than Bitcoin's and is capable of executing smart contracts itself. Moreover, Ethereum pursues a different goal: It is less about paying with Ether and more about building entire organizations on an electronic, decentralized basis.

Most Initial Coin Offerings (ICO) are therefore based on Ethereum. IOTA enjoys a lot of attention in the industry. This cryptocurrency modestly calls itself "the backbone for the Internet of Things (IOT)". This currency is intended to be used one day, when machines communicate directly with each other, to pay for services immediately without human intervention. These so-called machine-to-machine payments could be made, for example, by a car that pays the parking meter directly for the parking time as it drives away. Or a solar system that pays a frahling sensor for a forecast.

Unlike other cryptocurrencies, IOTA is not based on the blockchain. Still ahead of IOTA in third place on the ranking list of the largest digital currencies is another Bitcoin - Bitcoin Cash. This was created by a fork, a so-called hard fork.

This is the result of a change in the Bitcoin protocol regarding the data size of the blocks in the blockchain. Because the Bitcoin community could not agree, the split occurred. Every owner of a Bitcoin also received a Bitcoin Cash as of August 1, 2017. Litecoin was announced in 2011 as an alternative to Bitcoin. In the digital currency market, Litecoin is often referred to as "silver" and Bitcoin as "gold." Litecoin is considered silver because the Litecoin network can process transactions four times faster than Bitcoin.

Moreover, Litecoin's total supply is 84 million coins, while Bitcoin's total supply is limited to 21 million units. This quadrupling of the number of units means that Litecoin's potential inflation rate exceeds that of Bitcoin. How do crypto enthusiasts argue? Proponents are convinced by the democratic structure of the system and the lack of government control.

No central bank, for example, can intervene and finance the national debt via the printing press - and later inflate it. Thanks to the blockchain, the cryptocurrency Bitcoin and its sister currencies are forgery-proof and anonymous. Transactions with cryptocurrencies are faster and cheaper due to the elimination of intermediaries.

**How do crypto skeptics argue?**

Originally, the high volatility of Bitcoin and the absence of any regulation were the main reasons for criticism. The lack of value and susceptibility to technical problems are also often cited as disadvantages. Many skeptics now describe the market around cryptocurrencies as a Ponzi scheme. This is especially true since the number of new issues (ICO) has exploded and investors pay their stake with already existing cryptocurrencies. The price explosion of recent months alone shows that the market is in a bubble, he said. The cryptocurrency Bitcoin, which had set out to curb inflation, had triggered hyperinflation. Moreover, as the number of Bitcoins increases, the Bitcoin network system becomes slower and transactions become more expensive.

## What can I use Bitcoin or other cryptocurrencies for?

In Switzerland, Bitcoins can be purchased, for example, at SBB ticket machines or at comparable machines of financial institutions. Numerous stores, restaurants and online stores offer their goods in exchange for Bitcoin. However, these are often merely marketing campaigns. Given the high volatility, it is also difficult to define binding prices in Bitcoin. The majority of Bitcoin owners hoard the cryptocurrency in anticipation of further price gains.

A small proportion of transactions in Bitcoin are also likely to be made because it is possible to evade monitoring by government authorities.

## How does a Bitcoin transaction work?

Customer A purchases an item or product from Seller B. Instead of cash, A sends part of a bitcoin. If A and B have a smartphone and a crypto wallet is installed on B's phone, B can launch the software and receive a payment by scanning the QR code on A's smartphone. Immediately, A's account is debited and B's is credited. The transaction is sent to a peer-to-peer network around the world. Miners continuously scan the network for new transactions. Using hardware, the miners create blocks that contain a list of validated transactions.

These blocks are strung together in chronological order, creating a chain (hence the name blockchain). After about ten minutes, the transaction of A and B is confirmed by all computers in the network and secured in a decentralized manner.

**How can I purchase cryptocurrencies?**

The easiest way to access digital payment methods is via a so-called wallet provider. The first step is to create an account with one of the many wallet providers. As a rule, the personal details are verified on the basis of a credit card and ID copy. After a few minutes, you can transfer money via credit card and receive your Bitcoin balance. If you buy coins from such a provider, they will be managed there.

The insolvency of providers or hacker attacks have shown that the assets there are only partially secure - especially if the wallet providers are located in emerging markets. That is why you should have the coins "delivered" to you. Since they exist neither physically nor digitally (but only as a file in the blockchain), you only need the code of your coins, which shows you the way to the access code in the wallet. This code must be stored securely, preferably several times and on a storage medium that is offline. With the help of this code, you can access your Bitcoins at any time; if it is lost, the Bitcoin balance is also gone. Meanwhile, numerous banks offer accounts and products for investing in Bitcoin. These are expensive, but you do not have to worry about the security and storage of the codes. The services of the wallet provider are not for free either, especially the exchange back into traditional currencies can cost a lot of money depending on the provider.

The fee for a Bitcoin transfer usually depends on the load of the system. If the system is very busy, the wallet provider usually increases the fee. To buy cryptocurrencies, you need a wallet, i.e. a virtual wallet. It is used to store the digital coins and is the prerequisite for buying and storing cryptocurrencies and using them as a means of payment.

The wallets are a part of the access software for the respective network - so to buy different cryptocurrencies, you need a separate wallet for each. The digital coins are stored in a wallet in the form of algorithmic, cryptographically encrypted strings. The prerequisite for the generation of these "private keys" is the confirmation of the respective transaction and its deposit in the blockchain. A private key is obtained when digital coins of the respective cryptocurrency are received or sent.

It is the unique proof of ownership over the virtual money. However, you have to make sure that you do not lose the private keys for your transactions. In such a case, you will no longer have permanent access to this transaction amount, as the blockchain technology does not allow you to generate the private keys multiple times.

There are special security systems for "dormant" digital money that is intended to serve as an investment. As a permanent transaction address, which is encrypted, but in principle works like an e-mail address and you get a "public key" (public key) after opening your network access/user account. With this provider you can manage your coins offline:

www.trezor.io

**Should I invest in cryptocurrencies?**

So far, there has been no comparable price development on the capital markets that did not end in a dramatic price correction. This is likely to be the case with cryptocurrencies as well. But when the price correction will be the case is difficult to estimate. Never before has it been so easy to speculate with a scarce commodity over the Internet. Those who don't want to go too far out on a limb, but don't want to miss out on the speculation opportunities offered by the digital currency, will tend to go for a bank product.

Those who want to grasp and "feel" the technology will invest a smaller sum in Bitcoin and get started on the web. The volatility of the Bitcoin price can be exemplified by the period between December 7 and 10. The price shot up several times within hours and even minutes by more than 1000 dollars, only to fall again shortly afterwards in a similarly drastic manner, and in January 2018 alone, the price of Bitcoin & Co. collapsed by up to 25% in some cases, which corresponded to a loss of around 21 billion USD.

My suggestion would be, if you want to speculate on the rise of cryptocurrencies, to still pick 10 favorable currencies that are under 5 euros per coin or to look out for completely new issues and already invest in a cryptocurrency at the pre-sale. Here I would not use more than 1,000 euros per currency, as you must expect the total loss of the investment here.

A new issuer would be e.g. BDX-Coin. If you invest 1,000 euros each in 10 different young currencies, you will have invested 10,000 euros. Here you best not have to do anything more and just leave your coins in the wallet. If only one of the 10 currencies, gets an approximate success like Bitcoin, you would be a millionaire in a short time.

Only invest money here that you do not need and can also lose. If you invest 1.000 Euro at BDX-Coins in the pre-sale, you would get the Coins at 0.15 Euro per Coin, so you would have about 6700 Coins in your Wallet. If these have a value of 1,000 euros per coin in 3 years, you are already among the millionaires and can bag 1,000 euros x 6700 = 6,700,000 euros.

I have explained the investment in already well-established cryptocurrencies in a later paragraph. Investing in cryptocurrencies is definitely worthwhile in view of the price and value development of digital currencies. However, from today's perspective, investing in cryptocurrencies mainly involves speculation: Unlike for shares and other securities, there are no established valuation formulas for digital currencies as yet. This is particularly clear in the case of pure cryptocurrencies such as Bitcoin; in the case of Ethereum or Ripple, the entire business model of the respective platform also flows more strongly into the valuation of the digital currency.

Investing in cryptocurrencies is therefore a bet on the future - whether the outcome is uncertain is something investors must decide for themselves. However, there are several points in favor of investing in digital currencies: Cryptocurrencies are currently establishing themselves as an alternative to so-called "fiat money" - conventional currencies. In the course of the digitalization of financial markets and monetary transactions, their importance will continue to grow.

They are a component of a crypto-economy with very great potential, which is currently still in its infancy, but will revolutionize the economy and financial markets in perspective. They have the potential to replace conventional currencies at a later date.

After all, digital currencies have been officially recognized means of payment in Japan and Australia since 2017. They enable extensive anonymity and thus the absence of state or private-sector control if the repeatedly discussed abolition of cash should really come. Bitcoin in particular is currently by far the highest-yielding investment option on the entire market. For investments in the most important other cryptocurrencies, one can also expect considerable returns in perspective - in the case of Ethereum, this point has probably been reached.

If you want to invest in cryptocurrencies, the decision is whether you are interested in a long-term investment or want to profit from short-term price changes. In the first case, it is about holding your stocks of Bitcoin & Co. for the long term. Of course, you have to counteract if the exchange rates change negatively in the long term.

However, the prices of all cryptocurrencies currently show a very strong fluctuation range. For example, the exchange rate of bitcoin can change by several hundred US dollars in very short periods of time or even on one and the same trading day. So, for long-term investments in cryptocurrencies, you need a long breath.

**Invest in Bitcoin**

Anyone who invested in Bitcoin a few years ago can now look forward to immense asset growth. With its performance, it has outperformed all conventional currencies and all other investment models. Economists have calculated that the exchange rate of the Bitcoin grew by almost 8,800 percent between the end of 2011 and mid-2017. Bitcoins purchased for $1,000 in December 2011 were thus worth about $8,800,000 in early July 2017. In the meantime, the Bitcoin exchange rate has continued to rise.

However, investing in Bitcoin is worthwhile even today and despite the now high price of this digital currency. Almost all professional observers agree that the Bitcoin price will continue to rise. If you want to invest money in Bitcoin, there are other good reasons for doing so besides the rapid growth in the value of this cryptocurrency: Unlike conventional currencies, the money supply of the Bitcoin is limited.

This results in a permanent appreciation pressure against the "fiat money".

## How do you secure your Bitcoins?

Some of the readers have been invested in cryptocurrencies for some time and have been able to make a significant profit and now have a ton of coins in their wallet, others use Bitcoin and other currencies only for transfers and to do business and payments or receive remittances. Others accumulate their profits from the business in cryptocurrency. Sooner or later, however, all owners of a wallet have the same need, namely to secure their coins in the wallet against hacker attacks, insolvency of the wallet provider or against exchange rate losses, or to have their coins paid out safely in fiat currency.

## How do I secure my bitcoin property?

During my research for appropriate solutions for this, I came across the provider Bitgold Ltd. The business idea of Bitgold Ltd. is to **hedge your coins in gold**. I think this idea is absolutely recommendable and ingenious! Bitgold Ltd. buys gold for your coins and stores it for you in different vaults worldwide, independent of banks.

The minimum deposit period is 6 months and the minimum deposit amount is 250gr of fine gold, which is equivalent to approximately

12,200 euros at the time of going to press. Withdrawals can be made back to a wallet, bank account, credit card or even delivered in physical gold. With this service from Bitgold Ltd, you have thus solved several problems at the same time: you can hedge your Bitcoins for a certain period of time, you are largely protected against inflation and crises with gold, you can transfer the investment back to your wallet after expiration if you assume rising prices of the cryptocurrency, but you can also have the gold delivered. You have a secure withdrawal channel through which you can get your Bitcoins paid out with the right infrastructure through Bitgold Ltd. Especially for larger sums, it is advisable to take professional help in getting your coins paid out instead of just having your coins transferred to your bank account via the wallet provider without thinking.

I know of a few readers who have had significant problems with their bank for larger withdrawals that came directly from the wallet provider. Therefore, my recommendation is to only withdraw amounts under 10,000 Euros directly to your bank account from the wallet. Use the service of Bitgold Ltd. to secure at least 30% to 40% of your coins. During the storage period, you can then decide how you want to receive the payout. After a long conversation with Bitgold Ltd. I am convinced that the management has enough experience to help you with the payout of your gold. So you can't get any problems of tax or other nature here.

The payout via the connected credit card through Bitgold Ltd. is also highly attractive. Various solutions are offered here on how you can dispose of your capital without any problems. The problem you may get with direct withdrawals from your wallet provider to your bank account is due to the fact that most wallet providers are registered and based in offshore places and often have their corporate accounts established in tax havens as well. If you then get a large withdrawal to your local bank account from a tax haven, this could cause problems with your local bank. This is not so significant for smaller amounts, but should you deal with larger amounts, this can lead to significant difficulties on several levels. Relevant money laundering laws must also be observed here, in which corresponding reporting requirements are enshrined.

Another reason why you should hedge your coins with at least 30% to 40% via Bitgold Ltd. is that I still see a big uncertainty factor here from the regulators and the various governments, which was clearly evident in China and South Korea in recent weeks, which have banned Bitcoin. At any time, laws can be enacted in Europe that restrict the use of your wallet as well!

Considerable uncertainties mainly lie with the wallet providers, as you could see recently with the example of Wirex, Xapo, Bitwala and TenX. With these providers, you can only withdraw and cash out your coins with a connected credit card; a withdrawal to a bank account is not possible.

Overnight and without notice, the Gibraltar-based card issuer has received an order from Visa to cancel all cards issued to various wallet providers, effective immediately!

If you have a wallet with this provider, you are now sitting on your coins and cannot withdraw them from this wallet until the wallet provider has found a new card provider, which can take months.

If you do not have a second wallet with another provider here to transfer your coins to, you are blocked as far as the payout of your coins is concerned until further notice! This cannot happen to you at Bitgold Ltd. with the connected card, because this card is established completely independent of any cryptocurrency.

Imagine the scenario that suddenly there is a legal decision that you can only dispose of your wallet in a certain amount of, for example, 2000 euros per month. What good is it if you are a "Coin Millionaire" but then it takes 40 years until you can finally get your Coins paid out in full?

So you can see why I think it is absolutely necessary to hedge your coins. This is especially true if you trade in larger dimensions! Bitgold Ltd. offers itself for this and I think that the management of Bitgold Ltd. has recognized exactly the problem. It offers the appropriate service for this. I could not find a comparable offer so far.

Advantage with Bitgold Ltd. for German-speaking prospective customers is also that you can correspond here also in German language, which is not possible with many wallet providers and with many transactions in connection with cryptocurrency.

I also strongly recommend you to get such a wallet provider where you can switch your coins to different cryptocurrencies or at least have one or two fiat currencies to choose from to switch your coins to. Also, always switch your coins to fiat currency within the wallet.

Here you are then protected in case of a crash of the coin value. If, on the other hand, you want to speculate on the rise of the corresponding cryptocurrency, then you can of course leave your coins in the wallet. It can also happen that the wallet provider refuses withdrawals to some credit institutions because, for example, they have come into conflict with the law with the regulatory authorities because they have made their accounts available to companies that had gambling and other things in the service, as was the case with a few institutions in Germany in recent months.

I think I have now provided you with enough facts why I strongly recommend hedging your coins. You can see all the necessary information about hedging on the website of Bitgold Holding Ltd. itself:

www.bitgold.asia

Reputable wallet providers are:

Tastra: www.tastra.com
Wirex: www.wirex.com

# FOREIGN INVESTMENTS

**Corona pandemic or the age of asset protection?**

The coronavirus has been considered to be the cause of a pandemic since March 11, 2020. With each day that followed, it became clearer, first for financial market insiders and then also for investors: The "golden decade" from 2010 to 2019, which ran without a U.S. stock market correction of over 20 percent, is probably finally over! The answer to the question of the extent to which the "lockdowns" ordered shortly thereafter across Europe succeeded in permanently containing the virus, or rather the COVID-19 disease caused by it, still remains open. From an economic point of view, the measures, which even in this country can be described as borderline in terms of civil and human rights, generally left a trail of destruction in their wake.

A word on the "Germany lockdown": Both the "Corona legislation," often perceived by the general public as dictatorial and ad hoc, and its implementation, or monitoring and occasional punishment, by an executive branch that in many places was extremely autocratic, undoubtedly led to lasting skepticism, fear and uncertainty in large parts of the population.

## From the "Golden Age" to the Recession of the Century?

As a result of the distrust of legislators, which has grown on a broad scale from March to date and has often increased continuously, numerous independent economists now interpret even some positive economic headlines extremely critically. A prime example of this is certainly the "good news" of the supposedly enormous increase in the propensity to buy, which was celebrated in the media shortly before these lines were written in August.

Various recognized economists suspected as the main motive for the sudden "buying mania" primarily one: the consistent implementation of the prophecies of doom à la "The main thing is to get rid of the money and nothing like out of all capital investments, whose real value, after a sale, in the last instance but the state decides!

These arguments were clearly heard, at least since April, even from private small investors. Given that there are currently around 2.9 million unemployed and tens of thousands of jobs at risk in the future - the keyword being short-time work - the search for a plausible, alternative justification is indeed challenging, to put it mildly.

Since July, after two quarters in a row in which GDP has fallen, it has been officially established that Germany is in a recession of the century. From April to June alone, GDP fell by 10.1 percent in relation to the previous quarter - the most massive decline since quarterly calculations began in 1970! By way of comparison or as a reminder:

During the financial market and economic crisis in 2009, this economic indicator declined by only a single-digit percentage in several quarters.

### Global economic crisis and dark future prospects?

The pandemic had an even more dramatic impact in the "shareholder mecca" par excellence, the USA. Gross domestic product in the world's largest economy fell by an annualized 32.9 percent between April and June. The unemployment rate exploded from 3.5 percent before the crisis to the current 11.1 percent. The outlook for the future is also bleak. For example, U.S. Federal Reserve Chairman Jerome Powell is warning of a historic GDP slump and believes that a full economic recovery is unlikely unless the virus is contained.

Meanwhile, COVID-19 infection numbers rose sharply again at the end of June, following initial signs of recovery in May.

### Diversification as the top investor imperative!

What do all these figures, facts and bad news mean for responsible and long-term future-oriented investors? The primary goal of the coming years is undoubtedly asset protection - the solid foundation of which has always been a strategically well thought-out portfolio diversification! Until now, the ideal has been, for example, to diversify investments in:

- a proverbial "iron gold reserve",
- various equity funds and in
- Residential and Commercial Real Estate.

In "times like these", another option, if not an absolute necessity, is **to build up an additional "investment pillar" as quickly as possible in the form of an investment in a non-EU country.**

Cross your heart. Do thoughts of rampant inflation, a currency crash in the next few years, or even "just" the future legal regulation of foreign money transfers (with capital controls) and/or investments really all fall into the category of doom-and-gloom pessimism?

We think the Corona crisis so far has repeatedly taught us that suddenly the "impossible" can very well become reality virtually overnight. A perfect example was the reintroduction of European Schengen area border controls, which were still considered "unthinkable" during the refugee crisis. To remain solution-oriented at this point and directly link to our Southeast Asia project: What are the concrete reasons for investing in Laos?

**Why is a non-EU foreign investment in Laos becoming a new "crisis pillar"?**

During my research, I noticed one country in particular that is very suitable for a foreign investment, but does not appear anywhere on the radar, as it receives almost no international attention. I have always spent several months a year in Asia for the past 20 years as well. In addition to the big tiger economies, Malaysia, Singapore, Indonesia and Thailand, one country has always been in my focus here for years: LAOS PDR.

I always call this country the Liechtenstein of Asia. The country is small, quiet, pleasant people and is far from being a tax haven. There are many banks from Asia, New Zealand and Australia. Here you can also set up a company that can be managed 100% by a foreigner as a shareholder, and thus without a domestic trustee.

De facto, it is a developing country - but the emphasis is clearly on "development. Internationally recognized market observers and economists assess and describe Laos as clearly emerging overall. Due to the newly established Silk Road of the Chinese, Laos is the transit country per se and an immediate economic upswing is imminent. I predict an economic growth of 10% - 17% per year here in the next few years! I myself also have a house there and am invested in various projects there.

Both geographically, due to its central location with borders to highly potent trading partners, and strategically, the country is extremely well positioned. These prospects undoubtedly qualify the country as a first-class destination for the investment objectives described above. However, what is at least as important to us in this investment project as the economic background is the local people and environment.

**Promising symbiosis of investment, people and ecology.**

Already during the conception phase, professional friendly relationships with local partners were established. These showed the friendliness and joie de vivre, but also the proactivity and willingness to work of the partners. Incidentally, these are character traits that, according to our experience, we perceived in large parts of the Laotian population. In addition to the expressed desire for a reduced dependence on the "powerful" neighboring countries such as China and Thailand, the Laotians involved showed an affinity, if not an open-honest enthusiasm, for European and especially German corporate cultures.

The three main reasons are:

1. The high product quality awareness
2. The "holistic-life" working conditions lived in this country, which enable a corresponding quality of life, as well as
3. Our strong environmental awareness.

From the very beginning, we were aware of the expectations placed in us and the responsibility associated with them, and we were ready to accept them.

Since the outbreak of the Corona pandemic, we are finally convinced that it is time to recognize humanity and ecology as the top priority in any economic thinking and acting! From our point of view, commercially reasonable projects and a corresponding capital protection for investors are very well possible even under these conditions. The concrete investment project could represent a historical "small, big step" for Laos towards self-sufficiency in the food sector.

Subsequently, this innovative project qualifies in principle to become a showcase and motivational project for future foreign engagements. This developing country deserves a fair chance for the future.

At the website below you can get more information and also get in touch with German businessmen who invest there and thus can also point out appropriate investment opportunities.

www.laos-investment.com
info@laos-investment.com

Just mention the Corona Crash book as a reference and you will be served quickly and preferentially.

# THE WORLD MONEY SCAM

The whole financial system including all central banks was built up worldwide as a huge so-called Ponzi fraud system, which is now on the verge of collapse. This world money fraud contains in principle 4 stages.

Stage One: First, historically, there was the real money, namely coins of gold and silver, this was then replaced by bank receipts for deposited precious metal. Then criminal bankers started printing more receipts than they actually held in precious metals.

In stage 2, the banksters abandoned gold backing altogether and printed only counterfeit money. This allowed them to collect interest on gold they did not own at all.

Then came stage three: because they couldn't print this counterfeit money fast enough, and because they wanted to satisfy their boundless greed even faster, they started issuing so-called giro money, that is, electronic money that was only partially backed by cash. This is the so-called fractional reserve banking system, which is, of course, a fraud.

Now they want to give up this partial coverage by paper money, too, so that they can generate even more fiat money. The printing presses are simply no longer running fast enough for them. If they wanted to cover all the fraudulent financial derivatives with paper money, entire forests would have to be cut down for paper production.

In this way, these financial terrorists want to prevent too many of the idiot sheep from collecting their money from the bank at the same time in the event of a crisis and thus being able to bring it to safety. In the event of a currency reform, the sheep are not to get off scot-free under any circumstances.

Moreover, gold and cash is a form of financial autonomy because it protects privacy from state-terrorist criminals - and in a totalitarian, state-terrorist Orwellian surveillance state, this last surviving form of sovereignty and freedom cannot be tolerated at all. After all, sheep cannot decide when they are to be slaughtered.

Let's assume that Corona didn't suddenly appear, so it didn't come about by fate. It could also have been directed by interested circles. Read the following very important remarks on the financial markets.

In September 2019, the Fed in the U.S. injected massive amounts of capital amounting to several hundred billion dollars into the so-called repo market within a very short period of time. The reason for this was a near collapse of the global financial system. In the night of September 17, 2019, a certain interest rate, which is set when banks want to lend money to each other, exploded without warning. Normal would be a rate of 2%, this suddenly rose to 10%.

After a much smaller amount had been enough to prop up the financial system in 2008, this time it was all about the big picture. The banks' confidence in each other was thus gone. Only the extreme support purchases mentioned above, after the Fed had created the money beforehand, again prevented worse.

In January 2020, incidentally before the media coverage of Corona began, the Fed reported that emergency lending to the banking industry would continue unchanged. The Fed kept the names of the recipients secret so that, according to its own statement, the recipients could not get the reputation of being needy.

The Fed's total assets (i.e., the amount of money with which the central bank participates in the U.S. economy) have increased extremely over the past 1.5 years.

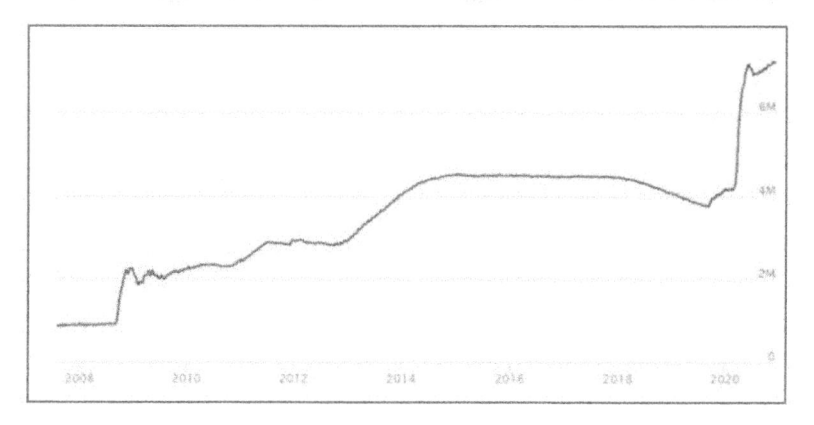

Die Entwicklung der Bilanzsumme seit 2008. (Quelle: Federal Reserve System)

While the Fed's balance sheet total was $3.7 trillion in September 2019 (before the last crash), it is now $7.24 trillion as of December 2020. In 2008, by the way, it had still amounted to about $1 trillion, as can be seen.

The financial market boom fueled by central banks is thus in its final phase. Since 1929, the Fed has never been involved in the U.S. economy to the extent it is now.

This brings back memories of the dot.com bubble in 2000, when investors were also externally positive and there was a record number of IPOs, just like in 2020. The difference this time, however, is that the real economy is in a bad way because of Corona, and yet stock market prices continue to rise.

Anyone who now believes that the extreme money supply exploitation is only an American problem is mistaken. The European Central Bank (ECB) also recently expanded its bond-buying program by 500 billion euros to 1.85 trillion euros. Together with the other monetary programs, the total amount of central bank money should soon be around 7-8 trillion euros. The euro zone is thus much closer to the critical limit of 12 trillion euros (gross domestic product GDP of the euro zone).

So the bet is no longer on whether the system will collapse, but when. According to optimistic forecasts, it will take until 2025, although 2023 seems to be a more realistic date. Crash prophets are not satisfied with that either, but see the big collapse as early as 2021.

So far, at any rate, no one has been able to explain cogently how the world is supposed to get out of this misery without hyperinflation. In a lecture in December 2020, H.W. Sinn calculated that the euro could end up with a devaluation potential of up to 84%.

However, there would be another solution, a managed digital central bank money. In this scenario, all commercial banks would be abolished or merged into 2-3 large banks, and every citizen would then receive a checking account at the central bank. This account will then be used for everything from grocery shopping to parking tickets to paying taxes. The previous money disappears completely. Of course, this goes hand in hand with complete monitoring of all citizens, including in the financial sphere. Whoever gains access to the central bank accounts will then also have an overview of the history of all money spent by citizens. The state will see all expenditures such as movie tickets, lollipops, purchases of alcohol, expenditures for plastic surgeons....

I think we have seen exactly where this total surveillance can lead. The state and the media will highlight the advantages of the new monetary system with a huge campaign (how this works has already been seen very well in 2020). In the first place, of course, this includes the simplification of all payment transactions, and in the second step, the significantly cheaper provision of all financial services. We are also moving more and more in the direction of a state in which the government, and no longer the citizen, determines what is best for everyone.

Currently, the process of money creation is accelerating even further. Clever contemporaries have been asking themselves two questions for some time:

1. Why doesn't all that money lead to rampant huge inflation?
2. When will the system break down?

I am asking a third question here:

3. Which investments are still safe at all?

Here's what to say about the first two questions:

At present, the new money created is essentially used for financial transactions between the respective central bank and the commercial banks. For various reasons, however, the commercial banks are lending very little. The new money thus hardly comes into circulation.

The entire financial system is based on trust. As long as citizens still have this trust, they will not go to their savings accounts to withdraw them, for example. Citizens' spending is also very moderate. More savings are being made. What we are seeing at the moment is a reallocation of spending on vacations and eating out to online purchases. So there is a very slow velocity of money circulation. So if guarantors' confidence wanes, they would take the money and invest it in other assets. At the beginning of the downward spiral, these are values such as real estate, stocks, gold and silver, and later on consumer goods such as computers, televisions, etc. In the end, everything is bought that looks somehow valuable. This happens at an ever-increasing rate. This behavior then leads to the aforementioned hyperinflation with extreme devaluation of money.

At the same time, the banks also lose confidence in each other and in the central banks, which then leads to the collapse of the monetary system.

No one owns a crystal ball to predict the future.

**Diversification**

The way out is clear, the international diversification described in this book, both in personal finances and for yourself as an individual. There are currently still plenty of ways to secure yourself internationally without emigrating. If you have read this book, in 2-5 years you will no longer be able to say that you did not know about anything!

# SECOND PASSPORT- WHY DO I NEED A SECOND PASSPORT OR CITIZENSHIP?

Imagine you wake up one day and you realize with horror that your so beloved free and democratic homeland with all the advantages of free capitalism or the so-called "Free Social Market Economy" has changed overnight into an ugly, communist and dictatorial state or even into a dictatorial and national socialist state comparable to the Third Reich.

Suddenly, from one day to the next, you can no longer read the books you would like to read, foreign newspapers are banned, and instead of RTL and BBC you can only receive the state propaganda TV program. Should you resist this paternalism, they will simply pick you up without a warrant and put you in an internment camp until you get better.

The access to any free lawyers is denied to you and when you have finally improved exclusively a supreme military commander decides, this can last then as a rule between 5-10 years, see Khodorkovsky or perhaps you also never improve! You will also be forbidden any travel abroad and your passport will be taken away from you and exchanged for a national ID card, with which you can identify yourself in your home country, but with which you cannot legally enter anywhere in the rest of the world, see North Korea. These scenarios existed in the Third Reich, at the time the Berlin Wall was built in the then resulting East Germany, in North and South Korea in Vietnam, Russia and

Burma (Myanmar), etc. You think this does not exist in our time? You are completely wrong! An example of this is Hong Kong. Since July 1, 1997 Hong Kong is suddenly no longer part of the western free world but is a special zone of the communist Chinese People's Republic. As a result, 6 million "Western" Chinese have tried to naturalize somewhere in the rest of the world. Not only the Hong Kong Chinese but meanwhile also many US Americans and Europeans are coming to the conclusion that in the turbulent times of economic and banking crises it certainly cannot be a disadvantage to build up a second foothold and thus a life insurance in another country. The reasons for this can be very complex:

- Maybe with your current passport you are a target for terrorists
- Perhaps you see the risk that your passport will be confiscated or not renewed
- You are afraid that your basic and human rights of your previous state will soon be further restricted or even completely disregarded
- You fear capital controls and restrictions from your state to move your capital freely
- You are afraid that with your current passport you might be subject to restrictions or bans on entering certain countries (e.g. if you have an entry stamp from Israel in your passport you will certainly have problems entering the United Arab Emirates and vice versa).

- Your previous passport requires too many visas, you cannot enter many countries without visas
- The passport of your previous state is unpopular and you get into considerable trouble every time you enter another country. You are treated badly and your luggage is checked in depth each time
- You can't invest where you want with your current citizenship and you have export restrictions
- You are taxed and exploited above average by your current state
- They are regularly called up for military service and military missions
- Compulsory testing, compulsory vaccination, extensive restriction of civil rights in connection with infection protection laws

and many, many more reasons...

**Normal ways to obtain citizenship**

You can basically obtain citizenship in most states by:

a) Birth
b) Naturalization by residence
c) Marriage
d) Adoption

e) Investment

There is not much to add to the process of obtaining citizenship by birth, marriage or adoption, except that you should seek the appropriate laws and requirements for this from your desired country of naturalization. These vary from state to state. Therefore, we will limit ourselves here to citizenship by investment or by the corresponding prescribed residence in order to then be able to apply for naturalization.

That you can find persons willing to marry and adopt for cash, depending on the country, I also do not have to explain to you. Here it is to be paid attention only to the fact that you do not issue powers of attorney on fortune or accounts or other possession to the dear ones, whom you want to marry or adopt and let, if possible, a notarial renunciation explanation, that the corresponding person cannot make any claims on you and has no claims on possession, capital and a future inheritance!

The normal process for naturalization by residence is very simple. You simply deregister from your previous place of residence and officially re-register in your country of choice. In most cases, this is done via a permanent residence visa, which may also be linked to a work visa, if you still have to work at all.

It is sometimes easier for certain sought-after professions such as doctors or engineers, or as entrepreneurs who create corresponding jobs, or even as pensioners or retirees. You should contact an appropriate lawyer who specializes in naturalization in your desired country or find any other intermediary.

In many countries, you have the option of simply backdating your entry and permanent residence by the prescribed years. You have then already spent the prescribed time in the country on paper and can now apply directly for naturalization without actually having to serve the prescribed period of residence in your country of choice.

If you do not want to use the small "clerical error" in your naturalization application to your advantage, you are of course free to take the whole normal version and serve your prescribed waiting period in your country of choice. However, there are enough people in most countries who specialize in inserting such "clerical errors" in your application, in exchange for small gifts.

Many countries also have so-called investment programs that can lead to immediate naturalization, including Brazil, Argentina, Dominican Republic and other countries.

Often, such investment programs are very short-lived and change depending on how the respective minister changes office. It is therefore pointless to list any specific programs here. Even the Republic of Austria has such a law, which allows naturalization with a minimum investment in the Alpine Republic of 1 million euros. Unfortunately, it was not possible to find out whether this sum had already been raised by the time this book was completed.

In Ireland, it's 10 million euros for naturalization. The Seychelles had a program known only to insiders. With an investment of 10 million US dollars, you were guaranteed immediate naturalization as well as absolute diplomatic immunity (you were probably allowed to reside in a villa converted into an embassy building, including special diplomatic appointments). We do not know if this program described above still exists.

However, it is also a fact that most legal naturalization programs were completely shut down after the 9/11 attacks due to great pressure from the United States.

**Economic Citizenship-the fastest way to a second passport.**

The following countries have legally established an Economic Citizenship Program: St. Kitts, Commonwealth of Dominica, Antigua & Barbuda, Grenada and St. Lucia, and the Pacific island of Vanuatu.

All these countries can be mediated by the following provider at good conditions, because this provider has direct contacts to the respective governments and lawyers:

www.camel-management.com
info@camel-management.com

**Paraguay and the residence permit**

Those who do not know Paraguay will be very surprised. It offers the best conditions for emigration. There are easy immigration conditions and many freedoms that make the country so attractive. In addition, Paraguay offers the highest fixed interest rates in the world, up to 18% on savings deposits, which do not have to be taxed.

**Why emigrate to one of the freest states in the world?**

Paraguay is a minimal state. The Paraguayan government is considered superfluous, corrupt and criminal by the majority of Paraguayans. For this reason, it is very difficult for the state to pass new laws because the locals vehemently oppose them. This can result in an arson attack in the Paraguayan Congress, as happened on 02 April 2017. This effectively prevents a sprawling paternalistic and welfare state. The state is kept as small as possible. Even if the Paraguayan state tries to restrict the freedom of its citizens, this is hardly effective due to the individual corruption of authority employees.

**Climate and weather**

The climate in Paraguay is warm. If you are thinking about emigrating to Paraguay, you should definitely be able to cope with hot temperatures. In Asunción, the average temperatures are 32°C in summer and around 22°C in winter. The north of Paraguay, also called the Grand Chaco, is a dry steppe landscape where mainly cattle breeding is practiced. The south, on the other hand, is relatively humid and is considered one of the most fertile spots on earth.

## Languages

The official language in Paraguay is Spanish. In rural areas, people speak Guaraní, the language of the indigenous people. 5% of the population speaks German, but the language is being forgotten for generations. There is another peculiarity in Ciudad del Este. There, Portuguese is mostly spoken in the markets, since many merchants and customers are Brazilian. If you want to live in Paraguay, you should be able to speak Spanish.

## The currency - the rock in the surf

Paraguay's Guaraní has historically had strong inflation. Over the past 15 years, it has been considered one of the most stable currencies in South America.

Conversion rate: 1€ = 8434 PYG (Guaraní, as of 11.01.2021)

## Euro and US Dollar

As you can see, the guaraní has appreciated against the euro by about 10% over the last 10 years. Against the U.S. dollar, on the other hand, there has been a 10% devaluation over the same period.

The Guaraní is stable in contrast to the inflationary currencies of its neighboring countries, whose devaluation and loss of purchasing power is staggering.

## Cooperative Banks (Cooperativas)

Paraguay's cooperative banks are known for their high fixed interest rates, example see picture below. Cooperative banks are also known from Germany, e.g. Volks- und Raiffeisenbanken. These are considered safe compared to the private banks such as Deutsche Bank, Commerzbank. While the big private banks were shaking badly at the time of the financial crisis in 2008, the Volks- and Raiffeisenbanks were able to make profits. This is also how it works in Paraguay. The cooperative banks work in the interest of their customers because they have a say in the goals. They have insight into the balance sheet. The cooperative banking principle is similar to that in Germany. Thus, these banks are considered comparatively safe. So far, no cooperative bank has ever gone bankrupt in Paraguay and they are constantly controlled by INCOOP (Instituto Nacional de Cooperativismo). INCOOP was founded by the cooperative banks themselves in order to be able to guarantee security of money and profitability.

For some German expatriates, this is an attractive way to generate passive income in Paraguay. Thus, many people live only from the high interest rates without having the compulsion to work for their money. Of course, the interest income is tax free for emigrants.

Now you ask yourself, where do these enormously high interest yields come from? The reason: the interest burden for someone taking out a loan is between 25% to 40%, because the demand is so high. The enormous interest gain is simply passed on to the investor.

**Tax haven**

Paraguay is considered a tax haven and is one of the lowest taxed countries in the world. Foreign income is not taxed at all and income within the country is taxed at a maximum of 10%. In addition, there is the possibility to offset all costs, even food purchases and not only business necessary expenses. Many small businesses are not registered, so there are no taxes. This is a good strategy for starting a startup. Value added tax is only 10%. It is also quite rare to pay this in Paraguay. Import taxes are the only taxes that are high. Importing foreign goods into Paraguay is therefore usually expensive.

**Economy**

In Asunción, Paraguay there is the new Porsche car dealership, the Sheraton hotel, the Complejo Blue Tower shopping center and a huge office building complex.

Agriculture in Paraguay is very dominant. From simple ox carts to highly modern agriculture, everything is represented. South of Ciudad del Este, you can see fields as far as the eye can see, cultivated with the most modern technology. In the western part and in the Chaco, cattle breeding dominates. The beef from Paraguay is considered one of the best in the world.

There are three major economic centers: Encarnción, Ciudad del Este and Asunción, all located in the southern part of Paraguay. In these three cities and around them, a huge service market is building up piece by piece, especially for trade and financial services. The official economic growth rate is around 5%. The number of unreported cases is probably much higher, which is difficult to verify, since many small businesses, as already mentioned, are not registered.

**What kind of work is worthwhile in Paraguay?**

As an employee, you hardly have a chance in this market. It is better if the immigrant directly becomes self-employed or an entrepreneur. In Paraguay, there are many things that are not yet available here. It would be enough to take some ideas from Germany and bring them to Paraguay. I learned locally that recently someone became very wealthy just by making ketchup. You can do that with many other things as well. Highly qualified craftsmen are also always in demand, since Paraguayans are considered to be not very precise in their work. There is no compulsion to be a master craftsman.

## Cost of living

The cost of living is about 1/3 of the German cost of everyday life. But be careful, for foreigners the prices are increased strongly. If you are not careful, badly informed or the language barrier is too high, it can become considerably more expensive. If you go shopping, you should know the prices beforehand! At markets it is generally cheaper than in the big supermarkets. The things that are comparatively costly are, as already mentioned, imported goods. Real estate prices are rising from year to year.

## Early retirement due to high interest rates

Anyone who wants to emigrate as a pensioner should take a closer look at Paraguay. If he has saved 60,000 €, he can profit from the high interest rates in Paraguay. Already with 65,000 €, which he invests in Paraguay, he gets 18% interest, which corresponds to a monthly pension of 975 €. From such an income the emigrant can live well in Paraguay.

## Medical care

In the metropolitan areas such as Asunción, Encarnatión and Ciudad del Este, medical care is not a problem. Only outside in the countryside it becomes more difficult. If you have health problems, you should not live too far away from the metropolitan areas. The quality of health care can be rated from medium to very good. Of course, the state clinics do not have the same quality as the private clinics. The private clinics have a higher standard than in Germany and first class medical care, which many wealthy locals appreciate. Among the very good clinics in Asunción are: La Costa, Centro Medico Bautista and many specialty clinics. The cost of health insurance is about 100 € per month per person with all benefits. If you are young and seldom ill, you should calculate whether insurance is worthwhile because the cost of treatment is low.

**Security**

Paraguay is considered a safe country in South America with a low risk rating. More information about this is available on the Travel Risk Map 2018. Unfortunately, the police is considered very corrupt and works quite ineffectively. In return, you have a high percentage of private gun ownership and the high density of private security companies that provide security. Only on the eastern border with Brazil is crime higher. Most of the crime is committed by Brazilians crossing the border, as in the $40 million robbery in Ciudad del Este.

## Self defense with firearms

If you are a gun lover and want to defend yourself, you should emigrate to Paraguay! The legislation here is very liberal. Anyone who has a cédula and a clean criminal record can buy a gun and use it on his property for self-defense. There is still a special gun license that allows you to carry the gun loaded in public. The gun license costs extra. Weapons are nevertheless relatively expensive in Paraguay, unlike in other countries, because of the high import taxes and the therefore more difficult import.

## Conclusion

If you love freedom and want to be confronted as little as possible with a state bureaucracy, you should emigrate to Paraguay. As an entrepreneur, this country offers the best conditions to open a business, due to low regulation and tax. In 2019, 409 Germans officially emigrated to Paraguay and 384 returned home. Within the 10 years from 2008 to 2017, 4,098 Germans officially emigrated to Paraguay and 3,667 moved back to Germany.

Only 7 million inhabitants live in a country area larger than Germany. By far the largest concentration is in and around the capital Asunción (about 3 million). Almost everywhere, more or less South American or, better, Paraguayan Spanish (mixed with some Guaraní) is spoken. Especially outside the cities, however, Guaraní is usually the main language of the population. Over 200,000 Brazilians live in the country, as well as over 50,000 Argentines. Other minorities come from Korea, Taiwan, Chile, Bolivia, Peru, Colombia as well as Spain, Italy and Japan. In the mostly remote Indian colonies, 17 different languages are spoken.

Paraguay is popular with retirees, self-sufficient people and people who love their privacy. About 5% of the population are immigrants of German origin or their descendants. The number of German speakers (Germans, Austrians, Swiss) varies. They range from a good 60,000 to about 170,000. Partially included in these calculations are some of the many (nearly 200,000) German Brazilians and the more than 30,000 Mennonites who also speak Low German.

The real estate prices are very favorable. There are numerous German-speaking doctors and service providers. Taxes are very low. There are few regulations and bureaucratic obstacles to becoming self-employed and carrying on any business. Little capital is needed to immigrate. Popular immigration areas are the Departementos Central (around the capital Asunción) and Cordillera as well as in the Independencia area.

In Paraguay, there are modern supermarkets and shopping centers with almost all products that are also available in Europe. Of course, the offer in the countryside is not so abundant. Also, the streets in some parts of Paraguay leave much to be desired. Order and cleanliness are not rated as highly as perhaps in Germany. But the people themselves pay scrupulous attention to good personal hygiene.

**Entry and immigration**

As an EU citizen, a citizen of Switzerland or an EEA citizen, entry to Paraguay is with a valid passport. Entry with an identity card is not permitted. Up to a duration of stay of 90 days, tourists from the above-mentioned countries do not need a visa.

With the approval of the Paraguayan immigration authorities, the stay can be extended once for another 90 days. Another possibility to extend the stay without applying for a permanent residence permit is to leave and re-enter the country for a short period of time. Detailed information on immigration can be found on the page Immigration Requirements. This entitles you to a 3-month visa-free stay in Paraguay, which can be extended once without having to immigrate or apply for a permanent residence permit and Paraguayan ID card. By leaving and re-entering Paraguay, you can also extend your stay.

In the national capital, Asunción, the permanent residence permit and the Paraguayan identity card (Cedulá) are applied for by submitting all papers and providing proof of capital.

A good starting point to explore Paraguay, to find a suitable property or just to spend your vacation and relax is the ostrich farm "Mbuni", run by a German couple. Here you can live in a tasteful and harmonious atmosphere, enjoy and experience many new things.

## Emigrate to Paraguay - Immigration Service

It is advisable to hire a professional immigration officer, otherwise it will be a very time-consuming and bureaucratic act for someone who is not very knowledgeable.

A reliable forwarder and immigration helper, fluent in German and Spanish, is Ademir Besteiro, who is a partner of OTC Global S.R.L., an experienced international forwarder. Here you can send your removal goods to Paraguay professionally and inexpensively.

## Special features and advantages at a glance

- No European stress
- No winter depression, because about 300 sunny days per year
- Green and blooming all year round, mostly warm weather
- Sun ripened tropical fruits from your own garden
- Life close to nature
- Low electricity costs, as electricity is generated almost 100% from hydroelectric power (no nuclear reactors)
- Very low property taxes
- Very low or no heating costs
- Politically, economically, war-wise uninteresting country (army of only 1,000 soldiers)
- No earthquakes or hurricanes

- Low population density
- Foreigner friendly residents
- Over 200,000 German-speaking inhabitants
- Some schools with German lessons, some German doctors, restaurants, etc.
- Affordable doctors and alternative practitioners (many natural remedies, herbs, etc.)
- Cheap maids, gardeners, etc.
- Simple immigration conditions
- Low capital needed for immigration, house, furnishings + car (from 50,000 euros) due to low land and construction costs
- No restrictive building regulations
- Low taxes (e.g. only 10% VAT)
- No taxation of foreign assets or income
- Uncomplicated commercial activity

**Paraguay - Immigration regulations**

**Immigration**

Immigrating to Paraguay for immigrants coming from Europe is quite straightforward (if you know your way around the Paraguayan bureaucracy).

As a rule, you enter the country as a tourist. A valid passport is required, which is valid for at least 6 months after entry. This entitles you to a 90-day visa-free stay, which can be extended once for another 90 days for a fee. In Asunción, the application for the permanent residence permit (Radicación Permanente) and, after receiving it, the Paraguayan identity card (Cédula de Identidad) can be started immediately.

**Immigration procedure**

Obtaining the permanent residence permit is preceded by several steps and administrative procedures. Therefore, it is good if you plan enough time for this before departure. Roughly, the to-do's can be divided into 4 categories:

1. Compiling the necessary documents in the home country
2. Application for legalization of documents in the home country
3. Compilation of the remaining documents on site in Paraguay
4. Submitting the documents in the immigration office in Paraguay

## Necessary documents

Below is a list of the necessary documents to be compiled in the home country. The original and a certified copy of all documents are necessary.

- Certified police certificate of good conduct for persons over the age of 14 (max. 3 months old)
- Birth certificate (preferably international)
- Marriage certificate (if married)
- Divorce decree (if divorced)
- Proof of liquidity: Proof of capital of a valuable property in Paraguay or deposit slip of 5,000 US dollars, or the equivalent in Guaraní, per family at a Paraguayan bank (to be done in Paraguay) or notarized employment contract with indication of salary.
- For pensioners the pension statement is required
- For school children the last school report is required

If you plan to practice a profession, you still need certificates and / or diplomas of professional training.

Send all documents in ORIGINAL to the Paraguayan Consulate General responsible for you with the request to legalize the documents. These documents, issued in German, will then be translated into Spanish by an authorized translator in Paraguay.

In Paraguay, it is advisable to use the services of an immigration consultant for the next steps in order to save unnecessary hassle and time. Together with your immigration consultant you now have to apply for the following documents:

- Current health certificate and Aids test (should be done in Paraguay).
- Affidavit of compliance with Paraguayan laws
- Proof of liquidity: proof of capital of a property of value in Paraguay or deposit slip of US$5,000, or the equivalent in Guaraní, per family at a Paraguayan bank.
- Certificate of good conduct for foreigners
- Registration certificate of Paraguayan residence
- Certified copy of identity card and/or passport (minimum validity of 6 months from date of entry)

Please keep in mind, if you are not fluent in Spanish, that you must necessarily interpose an agency that will fill out the documents and the applications, correct them and also submit them together with you. This complete service until you receive your cédula will cost you between 7,000 and 15,000 euros, depending on the professionalism and reputation of the local provider.

**Other countries:**

**You can never become a citizen of these states**

Naturalization and issuance of a passport of the following states should be almost impossible for you: Principality of Liechtenstein, Switzerland, Vatican, Monaco and San Marino. And not impossible but very difficult it turns out also for Thailand and Singapore.

# THE DIPLOMATIC PASSPORT

## IMMUNITY-TAX SAVINGS-POLITICAL CONTACTS-PRIVILEGES

Get a diplomatic passport and enjoy all the benefits mentioned above. Watch as doors open, taxes are reduced, and travel is made easier. A diplomatic passport and a diplomatic title open up a world of privileges and opportunities. Diplomatic passports are not sold. They are available to selected individuals.

### Become (Honorary) Consul

Consuls are highly respected individuals and important members of a community that is part of the elite diplomatic corps and, as such, offers privileges, protection and perks. They fly flags on their cars, never get parking tickets, drive in the fast lane at border crossings, have their own immigration desk at the airport, pay no real estate taxes, and have their homes and offices closed to law enforcement. They are recognized under international law and legally enjoy the same privileges as professional diplomats.

### What is an (honorary) consul?

Just like a consul, an honorary consul is an official representative of a state who is appointed to work in a specific state. It is different from an ambassador. An ambassador is the representative of a head of state in another country and heads an embassy, usually located in the capital city. A consul or honorary consul can head an official consulate in any city. His or her role is to strengthen relations, facilitate trade and investment between the two nations. The difference between a consul and an honorary consul is that honorary consuls are not paid.

### Who can become a (honorary) consul?

Countries appoint their honorary consuls based on age, experience, political and business connections, integrity, political views, and charisma.

### Diplomatic immunity and other benefits

Diplomatic immunity is a principle of international law under which foreign government officials are not subject to the jurisdiction of local courts and other authorities over both their official and, to a large extent, their personal activities. Their diplomatic immunity protects them from certain violations. Their bags are considered diplomatic baggage at customs and cannot be searched. Traffic tickets no longer apply to their cars. They do not have to pay sales tax on items purchased for their home and office. They do not have to pay property taxes on their home and office if they own the property. Their office and residence are inviolable territory of their sending country and may not be entered by host country officials such as police or army.

The benefits of a diplomat are agreed upon by 177 Vienna countries in 1963. It is called the Vienna Convention on Consular Relations. Each country interprets diplomatic immunity differently. There are many subtleties with which you should familiarize yourself.

*You can read the Vienna Convention on Diplomatic Relations in the appendix of this book:*

**There is no permission for illegal activities!**

Many people mistakenly think that a diplomatic appointment is carte blanche to commit illegal acts and they are protected from the authorities. Minor offenses, such as violations of traffic laws, do not result in the revocation of diplomatic immunity. However, more serious cases lead to the revocation of diplomatic immunity The receiving country may even request the sending country to revoke the appointment of the (honorary) consul.

Honorary consul appointments, as the name implies, are an honor and should be treated honorably by their holder. There are many cases where countries revoke honorary consultative titles for improper conduct.

## How to become a (honorary) consul?

One myth that we must dispel immediately is that honorary consul titles are sold on the Internet. Here, either stolen documents are offered or documents that have not been officially issued by the sending state. It may simply be a scam where you get nothing after a certain down payment amount.

To become an honorary consul, you must work with a diplomatic advisor, sometimes called a diplomatic broker. This person has a very strong international political network. Your advisor needs to know and understand your situation and intentions in order to provide you with the most appropriate option. A lot depends on where you live. If you live in New York or Geneva, it is difficult to become an Honorary Consul, as almost every country is represented in these cities. However, if you live in large cities of large countries (Houston, Miami, Toronto, Manchester) or capitals of small countries (Bratislava, Lisbon, San Jose), it is easier to make an appointment. Your background and history are important. You will need to submit a resume and essay with your application. Your sending country needs to make sure you are the right person to represent the country. Your status and education also make a difference. They need to see your education and your professional, scientific or business accomplishments.

**Ambassador at large**

**What is a special ambassador?**

A special envoy in general differs from an ambassador-in-residence in that he is not permanently stationed at an embassy. He represents his sending country in a region, a group of countries, or a particular international organization. For example, a special envoy may represent his or her country in the European Union, North America, or ASEAN countries. These positions do not have a permanent station and do not have the same privileges as the title of Honorary Consul, but do have a diplomatic passport and many other privileges.

**Honor and immunity**

International protocol requires that this person be addressed as His Excellency or Mr. Ambassador. The title also includes a diplomatic passport, travel privileges and diplomatic immunity. The sending country decides the specific roles of your status. You can be a dually accredited ambassador to two countries where the country does not have embassies, you can become an advisor to the Prime Minister based on your expertise, or you can represent your sending country in an international organization.

**Procedure to obtain a title**

The title for a Special Ambassador is usually much faster to obtain than the title of Honorary Consul, as you do not have to wait for the approval of the receiving country. You will need to provide us with your current documents (passport, birth certificate), professional resume, personal biography and additional supporting documents.

**Advantages of a diplomatic passport**

The advantages of traveling with a diplomatic passport are endless. Easy crossing at borders, special clearance at customs, and inviolability of luggage are just a few. You get protection of your safety and privacy when traveling to conflict areas, when your original passport would put you in danger. There are people who use a diplomatic passport to travel with sensitive documents that need to be protected from third parties. Here are some other additional benefits:

- Red carpet treatment and use of diplomatic lounges at many airports
- No tax liability on different sources of income
- Use of CC or CD or Consul license plates on cars.
- International prestige
- Instant door opener in political or business environments

- Meetings with high-ranking government officials possible in any country
- Sovereign inviolable status of your house and residence
- Free visas for any country and visa-free travel in many cases
- Departure tax at the airport is never due
- Diplomatic vehicles from Volvo and BMW with 20-40% discount (max. 2 vehicles per year)
- Travel upgrades for airlines and hotels.

**How to apply for a diplomatic passport**

Please note that diplomatic passports are not for sale. Any company or organization that claims to do so is fraudulent. A diplomatic passport contains several supporting documents from the issuing country and is registered with the Ministry of Foreign Affairs along with your appointment. Diplomatic passports are only available on a case-by-case basis.

**Those who are not qualified to become diplomats**

- Applicants with criminal record
- Applicants with international arrest warrants
- Applicants from international intelligence agencies

- Applicants who are high caliber but have questionable reputations
- Applicants under 30-35 years of age, unless they have achieved something outstanding

Only good things were also reported to us here by the company Elephant Consulting International Ltd., which we had already mentioned here several times and which is also very well networked. It can also show the appropriate and necessary government contacts:

www.camel-management.com
info@camel-management.com

Alternatively, you can also try this club, which, however, charges a membership fee of 9,500 euros, but can certainly help you through the very good contacts to appropriate members:

info@club-diplomats.vip
www.club-diplomats.vip

# SUMMARY

After studying all the chapters listed here, I would like to provide you with a brief summary to help you incorporate the points mentioned here in this book into an overall construct.

To do this, you should consider a healthy mix of all options to make the next months and years successful and safe:

1. If possible, change your residence to a low-tax country
2. Get a second citizenship with passport
3. If possible, keep as little capital as possible in bank accounts
4. Hold cash in USD/CHF/EUR/SGD/NWK
5. Invest at least ¼ of your assets in various foreign projects
6. Invest in land abroad where you can build and live yourself or practice agriculture. Make sure that you invest in a safe environment and that you are not an ethnic minority there, but that people from your culture already reside there.
7. If you are domiciled in a low-tax country, set up several offshore companies.
8. Try to have as many movable possessions as possible so that you can easily move from one place to another with your possessions in case of an emergency.
9. Reduce your real estate to the objects that are most important to you.

10. Invest in physical cryptocurrency, physical gold and physical silver.
11. Buy and store your precious metals abroad (Singapore, Hong Kong, New Zealand)
12. In order to guarantee your freedom of movement, the protection of your personality and your human and fundamental rights, establish a diplomatic position and/or a consulate (preferably abroad).

# EPILOGUE

With all this information I hope to have opened your eyes a bit now and I would be pleased if you take to heart at least some of these steps that have been listed here You can thus safely move into an uncertain future and create the appropriate protection for your family, your capital and yourself.

If you have any questions or need further information or advice on your plans, please feel free to contact me at the email below:

Graf-von-Staufen@protonmail.ch

# APPENDIX: Vienna Convention on Consular Relations Done at Vienna on 24 April 1963

The States Parties to the present Convention,

Recalling that consular relations have been established between peoples since ancient times,

Having in mind the Purposes and Principles of the Charter of the United Nations concerning the sovereign equality of States, the maintenance of international peace and security, and the promotion of friendly relations among nations,

Considering that the United Nations Conference on Diplomatic Intercourse and Immunities adopted the Vienna Convention on Diplomatic Relations which was opened for signature on 18 April 1961,

Believing that an international convention on consular relations, privileges and immunities would also contribute to the development of friendly relations among nations, irrespective of their differing constitutional and social systems,

Realizing that the purpose of such privileges and immunities is not to benefit individuals but to ensure the efficient performance of functions by consular posts on behalf of their respective States,

Affirming that the rules of customary international law continue to govern matters not expressly regulated by the provisions of the present Convention,

Have agreed as follows:

## Article 1
## Definitions

1. For the purposes of the present Convention, the following expressions shall have the meanings hereunder assigned to them:

(a) "consular post" means any consulate-general, consulate, vice-consulate or consular agency;

(b) "consular district" means the area assigned to a consular post for the exercise of consular functions;

(c) "head of consular post" means the person charged with the duty of acting in that capacity;

(d) "consular officer" means any person, including the head of a consular post, entrusted in that capacity with the exercise of consular functions;

(e) "consular employee" means any person employed in the administrative or technical service of a consular post;

(f) "member of the service staff" means any person employed in the domestic service of a consular post;

(g) "members of the consular post" means consular officers, consular employees and members of the service staff;

(h) "members of the consular staff" means consular officers, other than the head of a consular post, consular employees and members of the service staff;

(i) "member of the private staff" means a person who is employed exclusively in the private service of a member of the consular post;

(j) "consular premises" means the buildings or parts of buildings and the land ancillary thereto, irrespective of ownership, used exclusively for the purposes of the consular post;

(k) "consular archives" includes all the papers, documents, correspondence, books, films, tapes and registers of the consular post, together with the ciphers and codes, the card-indexes and any article of furniture intended for their protection or safe keeping.

2. Consular officers are of two categories, namely career consular officers and honorary consular officers. The provisions of Chapter II of the present Convention apply to consular posts headed by career consular officers, the provisions of Chapter III govern consular posts headed by honorary consular officers.

3. The particular status of members of the consular posts who are nationals or permanent residents of the receiving State is governed by article 71 of the present Convention.

# CHAPTER I.
# CONSULAR RELATIONS IN GENERAL
## SECTION I. ESTABLISHMENT AND CONDUCT OF CONSULAR RELATIONS

## Article 2
### Establishment of consular relations

1. The establishment of consular relations between States takes place by mutual consent.
2. The consent given to the establishment of diplomatic relations between two States implies, unless otherwise stated, consent to the establishment of consular relations.
3. The severance of diplomatic relations shall not ipso facto involve the severance of consular relations.

## Article 3
## Exercise of consular functions

Consular functions are exercised by consular posts. They are also exercised by diplomatic missions in accordance with the provisions of the present Convention.

## Article 4
## Establishment of a consular post

1. A consular post may be established in the territory of the receiving State only with that State's consent.
2. The seat of the consular post, its classification and the consular district shall be established by the sending State and shall be subject to the approval of the receiving State.
3. Subsequent changes in the seat of the consular post, its classification or the consular district may be made by the sending State only with the consent of the receiving State.
4. The consent of the receiving State shall also be required if a consulate-general or a consulate desires to open a vice-consulate or a consular agency in a locality other than that in which it is itself established.
5. The prior express consent of the receiving State shall also be required for the opening of an office forming part of an existing consular post elsewhere than at the seat thereof.

## Article 5
## Consular functions

Consular functions consist in:

(a) protecting in the receiving State the interests of the sending State and of its nationals, both individuals and bodies corporate, within the limits permitted by international law;

(b) furthering the development of commercial, economic, cultural and scientific relations between the sending State and the receiving State and otherwise promoting friendly relations between them in accordance with the provisions of the present Convention;

(c) ascertaining by all lawful means conditions and developments in the commercial, economic, cultural and scientific life of the receiving State, reporting thereon to the Government of the sending State and giving information to persons interested;

(d) issuing passports and travel documents to nationals of the sending State, and visas or appropriate documents to persons wishing to travel to the sending State;

(e) helping and assisting nationals, both individuals and bodies corporate, of the sending State;

(f) acting as notary and civil registrar and in capacities of a similar kind, and performing certain functions of an administrative nature, provided that there is nothing contrary thereto in the laws and regulations of the receiving State;

(g) safeguarding the interests of nationals, both individuals and bodies corporate, of the sending States in cases of succession mortis causa in the territory of the receiving State, in accordance with the laws and regulations of the receiving State;

(h) safeguarding, within the limits imposed by the laws and regulations of the receiving State, the interests of minors and other persons lacking full capacity who are nationals of the sending State, particularly where any guardianship or trusteeship is required with respect to such persons;

(i) subject to the practices and procedures obtaining in the receiving State, representing or arranging appropriate representation for nationals of the sending State before the tribunals and other authorities of the receiving State, for the purpose of obtaining, in accordance with the laws and regulations of the receiving State, provisional measures for the preservation of the rights and interests of these nationals, where, because of absence or any other reason, such nationals are unable at the proper time to assume the defence of their rights and interests;

(j) transmitting judicial and extrajudicial documents or executing letters rogatory or commissions to take evidence for the courts of the sending State in accordance with international agreements in force or, in the absence of such international agreements, in any other manner compatible with the laws and regulations of the receiving State;

(k) exercising rights of supervision and inspection provided for in the laws and regulations of the sending State in respect of vessels having the nationality of the sending State, and of aircraft registered in that State, and in respect of their crews;

(l) extending assistance to vessels and aircraft mentioned in subparagraph (k) of this article, and to their crews, taking statements regarding the voyage of a vessel, examining and stamping the ship's papers, and, without prejudice to the powers of the authorities of the receiving State, conducting investigations into any incidents which occurred during the voyage, and settling disputes of any kind between the master, the officers and the seamen insofar as this may be authorized by the laws and regulations of the sending State;

(m) performing any other functions entrusted to a consular post by the sending State which are not prohibited by the laws and regulations of the receiving State or to which no objection is taken by the receiving State or which are referred to in the international agreements in force between the sending State and the receiving State.

## Article 6
## Exercise of consular functions outside the consular district

A consular officer may, in special circumstances, with the consent of the receiving State, exercise his functions outside his consular district.

## Article 7
## Exercise of consular functions in a third State

The sending State may, after notifying the States concerned, entrust a consular post established in a particular State with the exercise of consular functions in another State, unless there is express objection by one of the States concerned.

## Article 8
## Exercise of consular functions on behalf of a third State

Upon appropriate notification to the receiving State, a consular post of the sending State may, unless the receiving State objects, exercise consular functions in the receiving State on behalf of a third State.

## Article 9
## Classes of heads of consular posts

1. Heads of consular posts are divided into four classes, namely
(a) consuls-general;
(b) consuls;
(c) vice-consuls;
(d) consular agents.

2. Paragraph 1 of this article in no way restricts the right of any of the Contracting Parties to fix the designation of consular officers other than the heads of consular posts.

## Article 10
## Appointment and admission of heads of consular posts

1. Heads of consular posts are appointed by the sending State and are admitted to the exercise of their functions by the receiving State.
2. Subject to the provisions of the present Convention, the formalities for the appointment and for the admission of the head of a consular post are determined by the laws, regulations and usages of the sending State and of the receiving State respectively.

## Article 11
## The consular commission or notification of appointment

1. The head of a consular post shall be provided by the sending State with a document, in the form of a commission or similar instrument, made out for each appointment, certifying his capacity and showing, as a general rule, his full name, his category and class, the consular district and the seat of the consular post.
2. The sending State shall transmit the commission or similar instrument through the diplomatic or other appropriate channel to the Government of the State in whose territory the head of a consular post is to exercise his functions.
3. If the receiving State agrees, the sending State may, instead of a commission or similar instrument, send to the receiving State a notification containing the particulars required by paragraph 1 of this article.

## Article 12
## The exequatur

1. The head of a consular post is admitted to the exercise of his functions by an authorization from the receiving State termed an exequatur, whatever the form of this authorization.

2. A State which refused to grant an exequatur is not obliged to give to the sending State reasons for such refusal.
3. Subject to the provisions of articles 13 and 15, the head of a consular post shall not enter upon his duties until he has received an exequatur.

## Article 13
### Provisional admission of heads of consular posts

Pending delivery of the exequatur, the head of a consular post may be admitted on a provisional basis to the exercise of his functions. In that case, the provisions of the present Convention shall apply.

## Article 14
### Notification to the authorities of the consular district

As soon as the head of a consular post is admitted even provisionally to the exercise of his functions, the receiving State shall immediately notify the competent authorities of the consular district.

It shall also ensure that the necessary measures are taken to enable the head of a consular post to carry out the duties of his office and to have the benefit of the provisions of the present Convention.

## Article 15
## Temporary exercise of the functions of the head of a consular post

1. If the head of a consular post is unable to carry out his functions or the position of head of consular post is vacant, an acting head of post may act provisionally as head of the consular post.
2. The full name of the acting head of post shall be notified either by the diplomatic mission of the sending State or, if that State has no such mission in the receiving State, by the head of the consular post, or, if he is unable to do so, by any competent authority of the sending State, to the Ministry for Foreign Affairs of the receiving State or to the authority designated by that Ministry. As a general rule, this notification shall be given in advance. The receiving State may make the admission as acting head of post of a person who is neither a diplomatic agent nor a consular officer of the sending State in the receiving State conditional on its consent.
3. The competent authorities of the receiving State shall afford assistance and protection to the acting head of post. While he is in charge of the post, the provisions of the present Convention shall apply to him on the same basis as to the head of the consular post concerned. The receiving State shall not, however, be obliged to grant to an acting head of post any

facility, privilege or immunity which the head of the consular post enjoys only subject to conditions not fulfilled by the acting head of post.

4. When, in the circumstances referred to in paragraph 1 of this article, a member of the diplomatic staff of the diplomatic mission of the sending State in the receiving State is designated by the sending State as an acting head of post, he shall, if the receiving State does not object thereto, continue to enjoy diplomatic privileges and immunities.

## Article 16
### Precedence as between heads of consular posts

1. Heads of consular posts shall rank in each class according to the date of the grant of the exequatur.
2. If, however, the head of a consular post before obtaining the exequatur is admitted to the exercise of his functions provisionally, his precedence shall be determined according to the date of the provisional admission; this precedence shall be maintained after the granting of the exequatur.
3. The order of precedence as between two or more heads of consular posts who obtained the exequatur or provisional admission on the same date shall be determined according to the dates on which their commissions or similar instruments

or the notifications referred to in paragraph 3 of article 11 were presented to the receiving State.

4. Acting heads of posts shall rank after all heads of consular posts and, as between themselves, they shall rank according to the dates on which they assumed their functions as acting heads of posts as indicated in the notifications given under paragraph 2 of article 15.
5. Honorary consular officers who are heads of consular posts shall rank in each class after career heads of consular posts, in the order and according to the rules laid down in the foregoing paragraphs.
6. Heads of consular posts shall have precedence over consular officers not having that status.

## Article 17
## Performance of diplomatic acts by consular officers

1. In a State where the sending State has no diplomatic mission and is not represented by a diplomatic mission of a third State, a consular officer may, with the consent of the receiving State, and without affecting his consular status, be authorized to perform diplomatic acts. The performance of such acts by a consular officer shall not confer upon him any right to claim diplomatic privileges and immunities.

2. A consular officer may, after notification addressed to the receiving State, act as representative of the sending State to any intergovernmental organization. When so acting, he shall be entitled to enjoy any privileges and immunities accorded to such a representative by customary international law or by international agreements; however, in respect of the performance by him of any consular function, he shall not be entitled to any greater immunity from jurisdiction than that to which a consular officer is entitled under the present Convention.

## Article 18
## Appointment of the same person by two or more States as a consular officer

Two or more States may, with the consent of the receiving State, appoint the same person as a consular officer in that State.

## Article 19
## Appointment of members of consular staff

1. Subject to the provisions of articles 20, 22 and 23, the sending State may freely appoint the members of the consular staff.
2. The full name, category and class of all consular officers, other than the head of a consular post, shall be notified by the

sending State to the receiving State in sufficient time for the receiving State, if it so wishes, to exercise its rights under paragraph 3 of article 23.

3. The sending State may, if required by its laws and regulations, request the receiving State to grant an exequatur to a consular officer other than the head of a consular post.

4. The receiving State may, if required by its laws and regulations, grant an exequatur to a consular officer other than the head of a consular post.

## Article 20
### Size of the consular staff

In the absence of an express agreement as to the size of the consular staff, the receiving State may require that the size of the staff be kept within limits considered by it to be reasonable and normal, having regard to circumstances and conditions in the consular district and to the needs of the particular consular post.

## Article 21
### Precedence as between consular officers of a consular post

The order of precedence as between the consular officers of a consular post and any change thereof shall be notified by the diplomatic mission of the sending State or, if that State has no such mission in the receiving State, by the head of the consular post, to the Ministry for Foreign Affairs of the receiving State or to the authority designated by that Ministry.

## Article 22
## Nationality of consular officers

1. Consular officers should, in principle, have the nationality of the sending State.
2. Consular officers may not be appointed from among persons having the nationality of the receiving State except with the express consent of that State which may be withdrawn at any time.
3. The receiving State may reserve the same right with regard to nationals of a third State who are not also nationals of the sending State.

## Article 23
## Persons declared "non grata"

1. The receiving State may at any time notify the sending State that a consular officer is persona non grata or that any other member of the consular staff is not acceptable. In that event, the sending State shall, as the case may be, either recall the

person concerned or terminate his functions with the consular post.

2. If the sending State refuses or fails within a reasonable time to carry out its obligations under paragraph 1 of this article, the receiving State may, as the case may be, either withdraw the exequatur from the person concerned or cease to consider him as a member of the consular staff.
3. A person appointed as a member of a consular post may be declared unacceptable before arriving in the territory of the receiving State or, if already in the receiving State, before entering on his duties with the consular post. In any such case, the sending State shall withdraw his appointment.
4. In the cases mentioned in paragraphs 1 and 3 of this article, the receiving State is not obliged to give to the sending State reasons for its decision.

## Article 24
## Notification to the receiving State of appointments, arrivals and departures

1. The Ministry for Foreign Affairs of the receiving State or the authority designated by that Ministry shall be notified of:
(a) the appointment of members of a consular post, their arrival after appointment to the consular post, their final departure or the termination of their functions and any other changes

affecting their status that may occur in the course of their service with the consular post;

(b) the arrival and final departure of a person belonging to the family of a member of a consular post forming part of his household and, where appropriate, the fact that a person becomes or ceases to be such a member of the family;

(c) the arrival and final departure of members of the private staff and, where appropriate, the termination of their service as such;

(d) the engagement and discharge of persons resident in the receiving State as members of a consular post or as members of the private staff entitled to privileges and immunities.

2. When possible, prior notification of arrival and final departure shall also be given.

## SECTION II.
## END OF CONSULAR FUNCTIONS

## Article 25
## Termination of the functions of a member of a consular post

The functions of a member of a consular post shall come to an end, inter alia:

(a) on notification by the sending State to the receiving State that his functions have come to an end;

(b) on withdrawal of the exequatur;

(c) on notification by the receiving State to the sending State that the receiving State has ceased to consider him as a member of the consular staff.

## Article 26
## Departure from the territory of the receiving State

The receiving State shall, even in case of armed conflict, grant to members of the consular post and members of the private staff, other than nationals of the receiving State, and to members of their families forming part of their households irrespective of nationality, the necessary time and facilities to enable them to prepare their departure and to leave at the earliest possible moment after the termination of the functions of the members concerned. In particular, it shall, in case of need, place at their disposal the necessary means of transport for themselves and their property other than property acquired in the receiving State the export of which is prohibited at the time of departure.

## Article 27
## Protection of consular premises and archives and of the interests of the sending State in exceptional circumstances

1. In the event of the severance of consular relations between two States:
(a) the receiving State shall, even in case of armed conflict, respect and protect the consular premises, together with the property of the consular post and the consular archives;
(b) the sending State may entrust the custody of the consular premises, together with the property contained therein and the consular archives, to a third State acceptable to the receiving State; the sending State may entrust the protection of its interests and those of its nationals to a third State acceptable to the receiving State.
2. In the event of the temporary or permanent closure of a consular post, the provisions of subparagraph (a) of paragraph 1 of this article shall apply. In addition, (a) if the sending State, although not represented in the receiving State by a diplomatic mission, has another consular post in the territory of that State, that consular post may be entrusted with the custody of the premises of the consular post which has been closed, together with the property contained therein and the consular archives, and, with the consent of the receiving State, with the exercise of consular functions in the

district of that consular post; or (b) if the sending State has no diplomatic mission and no other consular post in the receiving State, the provisions of subparagraphs (b) and (c) of paragraph 1 of this article shall apply.

## CHAPTER II.
## FACILITIES, PRIVILEGES AND IMMUNITIES RELATING TO CONSULAR POSTS, CAREER CONSULAR OFFICERS AND OTHER MEMBERS OF A CONSULAR POST SECTION I. FACILITIES, PRIVILEGES AND IMMUNITIES RELATING TO A CONSULAR POST

### Article 28
### Facilities for the work of the consular post

The receiving State shall accord full facilities for the performance of the functions of the consular post.

### Article 29
### Use of national flag and coat-of-arms

1. The sending State shall have the right to the use of its national flag and coat-of-arms in the receiving State in accordance with the provisions of this article.

2. The national flag of the sending State may be flown and its coat-of-arms displayed on the building occupied by the consular post and at the entrance door thereof, on the residence of the head of the consular post and on his means of transport when used on official business.
3. In the exercise of the right accorded by this article regard shall be had to the laws, regulations and usages of the receiving State.

## Article 30
## Accommodation

1. The receiving State shall either facilitate the acquisition on its territory, in accordance with its laws and regulations, by the sending State of premises necessary for its consular post or assist the latter in obtaining accommodation in some other way.
2. It shall also, where necessary, assist the consular post in obtaining suitable accommodation for its members.

## Article 31
## Inviolability of the consular premises

1. Consular premises shall be inviolable to the extent provided in this article.

2. The authorities of the receiving State shall not enter that part of the consular premises which is used exclusively for the purpose of the work of the consular post except with the consent of the head of the consular post or of his designee or of the head of the diplomatic mission of the sending State. The consent of the head of the consular post may, however, be assumed in case of fire or other disaster requiring prompt protective action.
3. Subject to the provisions of paragraph 2 of this article, the receiving State is under a special duty to take all appropriate steps to protect the consular premises against any intrusion or damage and to prevent any disturbance of the peace of the consular post or impairment of its dignity.
4. The consular premises, their furnishings, the property of the consular post and its means of transport shall be immune from any form of requisition for purposes of national defence or public utility. If expropriation is necessary for such purposes, all possible steps shall be taken to avoid impeding the performance of consular functions, and prompt, adequate and effective compensation shall be paid to the sending State.

## Article 32
## Exemption from taxation of consular premises

1. Consular premises and the residence of the career head of consular post of which the sending State or any person acting on its behalf is the owner or lessee shall be exempt from all national, regional or municipal dues and taxes whatsoever, other than such as represent payment for specific services rendered.
2. The exemption from taxation referred to paragraph 1 of this article shall not apply to such dues and taxes if, under the law of the receiving State, they are payable by the person who contracted with the sending State or with the person acting on its behalf.

## Article 33
## Inviolability of the consular archives and documents

The consular archives and documents shall be inviolable at all times and wherever they may be.

## Article 34
## Freedom of movement

Subject to its laws and regulations concerning zones entry into which is prohibited or regulated for reasons of national security, the receiving State shall ensure freedom of movement and travel in its territory to all members of the consular post.

## Article 35
## Freedom of communication

1. The receiving State shall permit and protect freedom of communication on the part of the consular post for all official purposes. In communicating with the Government, the diplomatic missions and other consular posts, wherever situated, of the sending State, the consular post may employ all appropriate means, including diplomatic or consular couriers, diplomatic or consular bags and messages in code or cipher. However, the consular post may install and use a wireless transmitter only with the consent of the receiving State.
2. The official correspondence of the consular post shall be inviolable. Official correspondence means all correspondence relating to the consular post and its functions.
3. The consular bag shall be neither opened nor detained. Nevertheless, if the competent authorities of the receiving State

have serious reason to believe that the bag contains something other than the correspondence, documents or articles referred to in paragraph 4 of this article, they may request that the bag be opened in their presence by an authorized representative of the sending State. If this request is refused by the authorities of the sending State, the bag shall be returned to its place of origin.

4. The packages constituting the consular bag shall bear visible external marks of their character and may contain only official correspondence and documents or articles intended exclusively for official use.

5. The consular courier shall be provided with an official document indicating his status and the number of packages constituting the consular bag. Except with the consent of the receiving State he shall be neither a national of the receiving State, nor, unless he is a national of the sending State, a permanent resident of the receiving State. In the performance of his functions he shall be protected by the receiving State. He shall enjoy personal inviolability and shall not be liable to any form of arrest or detention.

6. The sending State, its diplomatic missions and its consular posts may designate consular couriers ad hoc. In such cases the provisions of paragraph 5 of this article shall also apply except that the immunities therein mentioned shall cease to

apply when such a courier has delivered to the consignee the consular bag in his charge.

7. A consular bag may be entrusted to the captain of a ship or of a commercial aircraft scheduled to land at an authorized port of entry. He shall be provided with an official document indicating the number of packages constituting the bag, but he shall not be considered to be a consular courier. By arrangement with the appropriate local authorities, the consular post may send one of its members to take possession of the bag directly and freely from the captain of the ship or of the aircraft.

## Article 36
## Communication and contact with nationals of the sending State

1. With a view to facilitating the exercise of consular functions relating to nationals of the sending State:
(a) consular officers shall be free to communicate with nationals of the sending State and to have access to them. Nationals of the sending State shall have the same freedom with respect to communication with and access to consular officers of the sending State;
(b) if he so requests, the competent authorities of the receiving State shall, without delay, inform the consular post of the sending State if, within its consular district, a national of that

State is arrested or committed to prison or to custody pending trial or is detained in any other manner. Any communication addressed to the consular post by the person arrested, in prison, custody or detention shall be forwarded by the said authorities without delay. The said authorities shall inform the person concerned without delay of his rights under this subparagraph;

(c) consular officers shall have the right to visit a national of the sending State who is in prison, custody or detention, to converse and correspond with him and to arrange for his legal representation. They shall also have the right to visit any national of the sending State who is in prison, custody or detention in their district in pursuance of a judgement. Nevertheless, consular officers shall refrain from taking action on behalf of a national who is in prison, custody or detention if he expressly opposes such action.

2. The rights referred to in paragraph 1 of this article shall be exercised in conformity with the laws and regulations of the receiving State, subject to the proviso, however, that the said laws and regulations must enable full effect to be given to the purposes for which the rights accorded under this article are intended.

## Article 37
## Information in cases of deaths, guardianship or trusteeship, wrecks and air accidents

If the relevant information is available to the competent authorities of the receiving State, such authorities shall have the duty:

(a) in the case of the death of a national of the sending State, to inform without delay the consular post in whose district the death occurred;

(b) to inform the competent consular post without delay of any case where the appointment of a guardian or trustee appears to be in the interests of a minor or other person lacking full capacity who is a national of the sending State. The giving of this information shall, however, be without prejudice to the operation of the laws and regulations of the receiving State concerning such appointments;

(c) if a vessel, having the nationality of the sending State, is wrecked or runs aground in the territorial sea or internal waters of the receiving State, or if an aircraft registered in the sending State suffers an accident on the territory of the receiving State, to inform without delay the consular post nearest to the scene of the occurrence.

## Article 38
## Communication with the authorities of the receiving State

In the exercise of their functions, consular officers may address:
- (a) the competent local authorities of their consular district;
- (b) the competent central authorities of the receiving State if and to the extent that this is allowed by the laws, regulations and usages of the receiving State or by the relevant international agreements.

## Article 39
## Consular fees and charges

1. The consular post may levy in the territory of the receiving State the fees and charges provided by the laws and regulations of the sending State for consular acts.
2. The sums collected in the form of the fees and charges referred to in paragraph 1 of this article, and the receipts for such fees and charges, shall be exempt from all dues and taxes in the receiving State.

## SECTION II.
## FACILITIES, PRIVILEGES AND IMMUNITIES RELATING TO CAREER CONSULAR OFFICERS AND OTHER MEMBERS OF A CONSULAR POST

### Article 40
### Protection of consular officers

The receiving State shall treat consular officers with due respect and shall take all appropriate steps to prevent any attack on their person, freedom or dignity.

### Article 41
### Personal inviolability of consular officers

1. Consular officers shall not be liable to arrest or detention pending trial, except in the case of a grave crime and pursuant to a decision by the competent judicial authority.
2. Except in the case specified in paragraph 1 of this article, consular officers shall not be committed to prison or be liable to any other form of restriction on their personal freedom save in execution of a judicial decision of final effect.
3. If criminal proceedings are instituted against a consular officer, he must appear before the competent authorities. Nevertheless, the proceedings shall be conducted with the

respect due to him by reason of his official position and, except in the case specified in paragraph 1 of this article, in a manner which will hamper the exercise of consular functions as little as possible. When, in the circumstances mentioned in paragraph 1 of this article, it has become necessary to detain a consular officer, the proceedings against him shall be instituted with the minimum of delay.

## Article 42
### Notification of arrest, detention or prosecution

In the event of the arrest or detention, pending trial, of a member of the consular staff, or of criminal proceedings being instituted against him, the receiving State shall promptly notify the head of the consular post. Should the latter be himself the object of any such measure, the receiving State shall notify the sending State through the diplomatic channel.

## Article 43
### Immunity from jurisdiction

1. Consular officers and consular employees shall not be amenable to the jurisdiction of the judicial or administrative authorities of the receiving State in respect of acts performed in the exercise of consular functions.

2. The provisions of paragraph 1 of this article shall not, however, apply in respect of a civil action either:
(a) arising out of a contract concluded by a consular officer or a consular employee in which he did not contract expressly or impliedly as an agent of the sending State; or
(b) by a third party for damage arising from an accident in the receiving State caused by a vehicle, vessel or aircraft.

## Article 44
## Liability to give evidence

1. Members of a consular post may be called upon to attend as witnesses in the course of judicial or administrative proceedings. A consular employee or a member of the service staff shall not, except in the cases mentioned in paragraph 3 of this article, decline to give evidence. If a consular officer should decline to do so, no coercive measure or penalty may be applied to him.
2. The authority requiring the evidence of a consular officer shall avoid interference with the performance of his functions. It may, when possible, take such evidence at his residence or at the consular post or accept a statement from him in writing.
3. Members of a consular post are under no obligation to give evidence concerning matters connected with the exercise of their functions or to produce official correspondence and

documents relating thereto. They are also entitled to decline to give evidence as expert witnesses with regard to the law of the sending State.

## Article 45
## Waiver of privileges and immunities

1. The sending State may waive, with regard to a member of the consular post, any of the privileges and immunities provided for in articles 41, 43 and 44.
2. The waiver shall in all cases be express, except as provided in paragraph 3 of this article, and shall be communicated to the receiving State in writing.
3. The initiation of proceedings by a consular officer or a consular employee in a matter where he might enjoy immunity from jurisdiction under article 43 shall preclude him from invoking immunity from jurisdiction in respect of any counterclaim directly connected with the principal claim.
4. The waiver of immunity from jurisdiction for the purposes of civil or administrative proceedings shall not be deemed to imply the waiver of immunity from the measures of execution resulting from the judicial decision; in respect of such measures, a separate waiver shall be necessary.

## Article 46
## Exemption from registration of aliens and residence permits

1. Consular officers and consular employees and members of their families forming part of their households shall be exempt from all obligations under the laws and regulations of the receiving State in regard to the registration of aliens and residence permits.
2. The provisions of paragraph 1 of this article shall not, however, apply to any consular employee who is not a permanent employee of the sending State or who carries on any private gainful occupation in the receiving State or to any member of the family of any such employee.

## Article 47
## Exemption from work permits

1. Members of the consular post shall, with respect to services rendered for the sending State, be exempt from any obligations in regard to work permits imposed by the laws and regulations of the receiving State concerning the employment of foreign labour.
2. Members of the private staff of consular officers and of consular employees shall, if they do not carry on any other

gainful occupation in the receiving State, be exempt from the obligations referred to in paragraph 1 of this article.

## Article 48
## Social security exemption

1. Subject to the provisions of paragraph 3 of this article, members of the consular post with respect to services rendered by them for the sending State, and members of their families forming part of their households, shall be exempt from social security provisions which may be in force in the receiving State.
2. The exemption provided for in paragraph 1 of this article shall apply also to members of the private staff who are in the sole employ of members of the consular post, on condition:
   (a) that they are not nationals of or permanently resident in the receiving State; and
   (b) that they are covered by the social security provisions which are in force in the sending State or a third State.
3. Members of the consular post who employ persons to whom the exemption provided for in paragraph 2 of this article does not apply shall observe the obligations which the social security provisions of the receiving State impose upon employers.
4. The exemption provided for in paragraphs 1 and 2 of this article shall not preclude voluntary participation in the social

security system of the receiving State, provided that such participation is permitted by that State.

## Article 49
## Exemption from taxation

1. Consular officers and consular employees and members of their families forming part of their households shall be exempt from all dues and taxes, personal or real, national, regional or municipal, except:
   (a) indirect taxes of a kind which are normally incorporated in the price of goods or services;
   (b) dues or taxes on private immovable property situated in the territory of the receiving State, subject to the provisions of article 32;
   (c) estate, succession or inheritance duties, and duties on transfers, levied by the receiving State, subject to the provisions of paragraph (b) of article 51;
   (d) dues and taxes on private income, including capital gains, having its source in the receiving State and capital taxes relating to investments made in commercial or financial undertakings in the receiving State;
   (e) charges levied for specific services rendered;
   (f) registration, court or record fees, mortgage dues and stamp duties, subject to the provisions of article 32.

2. Members of the service staff shall be exempt from dues and taxes on the wages which they receive for their services.
3. Members of the consular post who employ persons whose wages or salaries are not exempt from income tax in the receiving State shall observe the obligations which the laws and regulations of that State impose upon employers concerning the levying of income tax.

## Article 50
### Exemption from customs duties and inspection

1. The receiving State shall, in accordance with such laws and regulations as it may adopt, permit entry of and grant exemption from all customs duties, taxes, and related charges other than charges for storage, cartage and similar services, on:
   (a) articles for the official use of the consular post;
   (b) articles for the personal use of a consular officer or members of his family forming part of his household, including articles intended for his establishment. The articles intended for consumption shall not exceed the quantities necessary for direct utilization by the persons concerned.
2. Consular employees shall enjoy the privileges and exemptions specified in paragraph 1 of this article in respect of articles imported at the time of first installation.

3. Personal baggage accompanying consular officers and members of their families forming part of their households shall be exempt from inspection. It may be inspected only if there is serious reason to believe that it contains articles other than those referred to in subparagraph (b) of paragraph 1 of this article, or articles the import or export of which is prohibited by the laws and regulations of the receiving State or which are subject to its quarantine laws and regulations. Such inspection shall be carried out in the presence of the consular officer or member of his family concerned.

## Article 51
### Estate of a member of the consular post or of a member of his family

In the event of the death of a member of the consular post or of a member of his family forming part of his household, the receiving State:

(a) shall permit the export of the movable property of the deceased, with the exception of any such property acquired in the receiving State the export of which was prohibited at the time of his death;

(b) shall not levy national, regional or municipal estate, succession or inheritance duties, and duties on transfers, on movable property the presence of which in the receiving State was due solely to the presence in that State of the deceased as a member of the consular post or as a member of the family of a member of the consular post.

## Article 52
### Exemption from personal services and contributions

The receiving State shall exempt members of the consular post and members of their families forming part of their households from all personal services, from all public service of any kind whatsoever, and from military obligations such as those connected with requisitioning, military contributions and billeting.

## Article 53
### Beginning and end of consular privileges and immunities

1. Every member of the consular post shall enjoy the privileges and immunities provided in the present Convention from the moment he enters the territory of the receiving State on proceeding to take up his post or, if already in its territory, from the moment when he enters on his duties with the consular post.
2. Members of the family of a member of the consular post forming part of his household and members of his private staff shall receive the privileges and immunities provided in the

present Convention from the date from which he enjoys privileges and immunities in accordance with paragraph 1 of this article or from the date of their entry into the territory of the receiving State or from the date of their becoming a member of such family or private staff, whichever is the latest.

3. When the functions of a member of the consular post have come to an end, his privileges and immunities and those of a member of his family forming part of his household or a member of his private staff shall normally cease at the moment when the person concerned leaves the receiving State or on the expiry of a reasonable period in which to do so, whichever is the sooner, but shall subsist until that time, even in case of armed conflict. In the case of the persons referred to in paragraph 2 of this article, their privileges and immunities shall come to an end when they cease to belong to the household or to be in the service of a member of the consular post provided, however, that if such persons intend leaving the receiving State within a reasonable period thereafter, their privileges and immunities shall subsist until the time of their departure.

4. However, with respect to acts performed by a consular officer or a consular employee in the exercise of his functions, immunity from jurisdiction shall continue to subsist without limitation of time.

5. In the event of the death of a member of the consular post, the members of his family forming part of his household shall

continue to enjoy the privileges and immunities accorded to them until they leave the receiving State or until the expiry of a reasonable period enabling them to do so, whichever is the sooner.

## Article 54
## Obligations of third States

1. If a consular officer passes through or is in the territory of a third State, which has granted him a visa if a visa was necessary, while proceeding to take up or return to his post or when returning to the sending State, the third State shall accord to him all immunities provided for by the other articles of the present Convention as may be required to ensure his transit or return. The same shall apply in the case of any member of his family forming part of his household enjoying such privileges and immunities who are accompanying the consular officer or travelling separately to join him or to return to the sending State.
2. In circumstances similar to those specified in paragraph 1 of this article, third States shall not hinder the transit through their territory of other members of the consular post or of members of their families forming part of their households.
3. Third States shall accord to official correspondence and to other official communications in transit, including messages in code

or cipher, the same freedom and protection as the receiving State is bound to accord under the present Convention. They shall accord to consular couriers who have been granted a visa, if a visa was necessary, and to consular bags in transit, the same inviolability and protection as the receiving State is bound to accord under the present Convention.

4. The obligations of third States under paragraphs 1, 2 and 3 of this article shall also apply to the persons mentioned respectively in those paragraphs, and to official communications and to consular bags, whose presence in the territory of the third State is due to force majeure.

## Article 55
### Respect for the laws and regulations of the receiving State

1. Without prejudice to their privileges and immunities, it is the duty of all persons enjoying such privileges and immunities to respect the laws and regulations of the receiving State. They also have a duty not to interfere in the internal affairs of the State.
2. The consular premises shall not be used in any manner incompatible with the exercise of consular functions.
3. The provisions of paragraph 2 of this article shall not exclude the possibility of offices of other institutions or agencies being installed in part of the building in which the consular premises

are situated, provided that the premises assigned to them are separate from those used by the consular post. In that event, the said offices shall not, for the purposes of the present Convention, be considered to form part of the consular premises.

## Article 56
## Insurance against third party risks

Members of the consular post shall comply with any requirements imposed by the laws and regulations of the receiving State, in respect of insurance against third party risks arising from the use of any vehicle, vessel or aircraft.

## Article 57
## Special provisions concerning private gainful occupation

1. Career consular officers shall not carry on for personal profit any professional or commercial activity in the receiving State.
2. Privileges and immunities provided in this chapter shall not be accorded:
(a) to consular employees or to members of the service staff who carry on any private gainful occupation in the receiving State;

(b) to members of the family of a person referred to in subparagraph (a) of this paragraph or to members of his private staff;

(c) to members of the family of a member of a consular post who themselves carry on any private gainful occupation in the receiving State.

## CHAPTER III.
## REGIME RELATING TO HONORARY CONSULAR OFFICERS AND CONSULAR POSTS HEADED BY SUCH OFFICERS

### Article 58
### General provisions relating to facilities, privileges and immunities

1. Articles 28, 29, 30, 34, 35, 36, 37, 38 and 39, paragraph 3 of article 54 and paragraphs 2 and 3 of article 55 shall apply to consular posts headed by an honorary consular officer. In addition, the facilities, privileges and immunities of such consular posts shall be governed by articles 59, 60, 61 and 62.
2. Articles 42 and 43, paragraph 3 of article 44, articles 45 and 53 and paragraph 1 of article 55 shall apply to honorary consular officers. In addition, the facilities, privileges and immunities of such consular officers shall be governed by articles 63, 64, 65, 66 and 67.

3. Privileges and immunities provided in the present Convention shall not be accorded to members of the family of an honorary consular officer or of a consular employee employed at a consular post headed by an honorary consular officer.

4. The exchange of consular bags between two consular posts headed by honorary consular officers in different States shall not be allowed without the consent of the two receiving States concerned.

## Article 59
### Protection of the consular premises

The receiving State shall take such steps as may be necessary to protect the consular premises of a consular post headed by an honorary consular officer against any intrusion or damage and to prevent any disturbance of the peace of the consular post or impairment of its dignity.

## Article 60
### Exemption from taxation of consular premises

1. Consular premises of a consular post headed by an honorary consular officer of which the sending State is the owner or lessee shall be exempt from all national, regional or municipal

dues and taxes whatsoever, other than such as represent payment for specific services rendered.

2. The exemption from taxation referred to in paragraph I of this article shall not apply to such dues and taxes if, under the laws and regulations of the receiving State, they are payable by the person who contracted with the sending State.

## Article 61
## Inviolability of consular archives and documents

The consular archives and documents of a consular post headed by an honorary consular officer shall be inviolable at all times and wherever they may be, provided that they are kept separate from other papers and documents and, in particular, from the private correspondence of the head of a consular post and of any person working with him, and from the materials, books or documents relating to their profession or trade.

## Article 62
## Exemption from customs duties

The receiving State shall, in accordance with such laws and regulations as it may adopt, permit entry of, and grant exemption from all customs duties, taxes, and related charges other than charges for storage, cartage and similar services on the following articles, provided that they are for the official use of a consular post headed by an honorary consular officer: coats-of-arms, flags, signboards, seals and stamps, books, official printed matter, office furniture, office equipment and similar articles supplied by or at the instance of the sending State to the consular post.

## Article 63
## Criminal proceedings

If criminal proceedings are instituted against an honorary consular officer, he must appear before the competent authorities. Nevertheless, the proceedings shall be conducted with the respect due to him by reason of his official position and, except when he is under arrest or detention, in a manner which will hamper the exercise of consular functions as little as possible. When it has become necessary to detain an honorary consular officer, the proceedings against him shall be instituted with the minimum of delay.

## Article 64
## Protection of honorary consular officers

The receiving State is under a duty to accord to an honorary consular officer such protection as may be required by reason of his official position.

## Article 65
## Exemption from registration of aliens and residence permits

Honorary consular officers, with the exception of those who carry on for personal profit any professional or commercial activity in the receiving State, shall be exempt from all obligations under the laws and regulations of the receiving State in regard to the registration of aliens and residence permits.

## Article 66
## Exemption from taxation

An honorary consular officer shall be exempt from all dues and taxes on the remuneration and emoluments which he receives from the sending State in respect of the exercise of consular functions.

## Article 67
## Exemption from personal services and contributions

The receiving State shall exempt honorary consular officers from all personal services and from all public services of any kind whatsoever and from military obligations such as those connected with requisitioning, military contributions and billeting.

## Article 68
## Optional character of the institution of honorary consular officers

Each State is free to decide whether it will appoint or receive honorary consular officers.

## CHAPTER IV.
## GENERAL PROVISIONS

## Article 69
## Consular agents who are not heads of consular posts

1. Each State is free to decide whether it will establish or admit consular agencies conducted by consular agents not designated as heads of consular post by the sending State.
2. The conditions under which the consular agencies referred to in paragraph 1 of this article may carry on their activities and the privileges and immunities which may be enjoyed by the consular agents in charge of them shall be determined by agreement between the sending State and the receiving State.

## Article 70
## Exercise of consular functions by diplomatic missions

1. The provisions of the present Convention apply also, so far as the context permits, to the exercise of consular functions by a diplomatic mission.
2. The names of members of a diplomatic mission assigned to the consular section or otherwise charged with the exercise of the consular functions of the mission shall be notified to the Ministry for Foreign Affairs of the receiving State or to the authority designated by that Ministry.
3. In the exercise of consular functions a diplomatic mission may address:
(a) the local authorities of the consular district;
(b) the central authorities of the receiving State if this is allowed by the laws, regulations and usages of the receiving State or by relevant international agreements.
4. The privileges and immunities of the members of a diplomatic mission referred to in paragraph 2 of this article shall continue to be governed by the rules of international law concerning diplomatic relations.

## Article 71

## Nationals or permanent residents of the receiving State

1. Except insofar as additional facilities, privileges and immunities may be granted by the receiving State, consular officers who are nationals of or permanently resident in the receiving State shall enjoy only immunity from jurisdiction and personal inviolability in respect of official acts performed in the exercise of their functions, and the privileges provided in paragraph 3 of article 44. So far as these consular officers are concerned, the receiving State shall likewise be bound by the obligation laid down in article 42. If criminal proceedings are instituted against such a consular officer, the proceedings shall, except when he is under arrest or detention, be conducted in a manner which will hamper the exercise of consular functions as little as possible.

2. Other members of the consular post who are nationals of or permanently resident in the receiving State and members of their families, as well as members of the families of consular officers referred to in paragraph 1 of this article, shall enjoy facilities, privileges and immunities only insofar as these are granted to them by the receiving State. Those members of the families of members of the consular post and those members of the private staff who are themselves nationals of or permanently resident in the receiving State shall likewise enjoy

facilities, privileges and immunities only insofar as these are granted to them by the receiving State. The receiving State shall, however, exercise its jurisdiction over those persons in such a way as not to hinder unduly the performance of the functions of the consular post.

## Article 72
## Non-discrimination

1. In the application of the provisions of the present Convention the receiving State shall not discriminate as between States.
2. However, discrimination shall not be regarded as taking place:
(a) where the receiving State applies any of the provisions of the present Convention restrictively because of a restrictive application of that provision to its consular posts in the sending State;
(b) where by custom or agreement States extend to each other more favourable treatment than is required by the provisions of the present Convention.

## Article 73
## Relationship between the present Convention and other international agreements

1. The provisions of the present Convention shall not affect other international agreements in force as between States Parties to them.
2. Nothing in the present Convention shall preclude States from concluding international agreements confirming or supplementing or extending or amplifying the provisions thereof.

## CHAPTER V.
## FINAL PROVISIONS

## Article 74
## Signature

The present Convention shall be open for signature by all States Members of the United Nations or of any of the specialized agencies or Parties to the Statute of the International Court of Justice, and by any other State invited by the General Assembly of the United Nations to become a Party to the Convention, as follows: until 31 October 1963 at the Federal Ministry for Foreign Affairs of the Republic of

Austria and subsequently, until 31 March 1964, at the United Nations Headquarters in New York.

## Article 75
## Ratification

The present Convention is subject to ratification. The instruments of ratification shall be deposited with the Secretary-General of the United Nations.

## Article 76
## Accession

The present Convention shall remain open for accession by any State belonging to any of the four categories mentioned in article 74. The instruments of accession shall be deposited with the SecretaryGeneral of the United Nations.

## Article 77
## Entry into force

1. The present Convention shall enter into force on the thirtieth day following the date of deposit of the twenty-second instrument of ratification or accession with the Secretary-General of the United Nations.

2. For each State ratifying or acceding to the Convention after the deposit of the twenty-second instrument of ratification or accession, the Convention shall enter into force on the thirtieth day after deposit by such State of its instrument of ratification or accession.

## Article 78
## Notifications by the Secretary-General

The Secretary-General of the United Nations shall inform all States belonging to any of the four categories mentioned in article 74:

(a) of signatures to the present Convention and of the deposit of instruments of ratification or accession, in accordance with articles 74, 75 and 76;

(b) of the date on which the present Convention will enter into force, in accordance with article 77.

## Article 79
## Authentic texts

The original of the present Convention, of which the Chinese, English, French, Russian and Spanish texts are equally authentic, shall be deposited with the Secretary-General of the United Nations, who shall send certified copies thereof to all States belonging to any of the four categories mentioned in article 74.

IN WITNESS WHEREOF the undersigned Plenipotentiaries, being duly authorized thereto by their respective Governments, have signed the present Convention.

DONE at Vienna this twenty-fourth day of April, one thousand nine hundred and sixty-three.

# APPENDIX: Vienna Convention on Diplomatic Relations Done at Vienna on 18 April 1961

The States Parties to the present Convention,

Recalling that peoples of all nations from ancient times have recognized the status of diplomatic agents,

Having in mind the purposes and principles of the Charter of the United Nations concerning the sovereign equality of States, the maintenance of international peace and security, and the promotion of friendly relations among nations,

Believing that an international convention on diplomatic intercourse, privileges and immunities would contribute to the development of friendly relations among nations, irrespective of their differing constitutional and social systems,

Realizing that the purpose of such privileges and immunities is not to benefit individuals but to ensure the efficient performance of the functions of diplomatic missions as representing States,

Affirming that the rules of customary international law should continue to govern questions not expressly regulated by the provisions of the present Convention,

Have agreed as follows:

**Article 1**

For the purpose of the present Convention, the following expressions shall have the meanings hereunder assigned to them:
(a) The "head of the mission" is the person charged by the sending State with the duty of acting in that capacity;
(b) The "members of the mission" are the head of the mission and the members of the staff of the mission;
(c) The "members of the staff of the mission" are the members of the diplomatic staff, of the administrative and technical staff and of the service staff of the mission;
(d) The "members of the diplomatic staff" are the members of the staff of the mission having diplomatic rank;
(e) A "diplomatic agent" is the head of the mission or a member of the diplomatic staff of the mission;
(f) The "members of the administrative and technical staff" are the members of the staff of the mission employed in the administrative and technical service of the mission;
(g) The "members of the service staff" are the members of the staff of the mission in the domestic service of the mission;
(h) A "private servant" is a person who is in the domestic service of a member of the mission and who is not an employee of the sending State;

(i) The "premises of the mission" are the buildings or parts of buildings and the land ancillary thereto, irrespective of ownership, used for the purposes of the mission including the residence of the head of the mission.

## Article 2

The establishment of diplomatic relations between States, and of permanent diplomatic missions, takes place by mutual consent.

## Article 3

1. The functions of a diplomatic mission consist, inter alia, in:
(a) Representing the sending State in the receiving State;
(b) Protecting in the receiving State the interests of the sending State and of its nationals, within the limits permitted by international law;
(c) Negotiating with the Government of the receiving State;
(d) Ascertaining by all lawful means conditions and developments in the receiving State, and reporting thereon to the Government of the sending State;
(e) Promoting friendly relations between the sending State and the receiving State, and developing their economic, cultural and scientific relations.

2. Nothing in the present Convention shall be construed as preventing the performance of consular functions by a diplomatic mission.

## Article 4

1. The sending State must make certain that the agrément of the receiving State has been given for the person it proposes to accredit as head of the mission to that State.
2. The receiving State is not obliged to give reasons to the sending State for a refusal of agrément.

## Article 5

1. The sending State may, after it has given due notification to the receiving States concerned, accredit a head of mission or assign any member of the diplomatic staff, as the case may be, to more than one State, unless there is express objection by any of the receiving States.
2. If the sending State accredits a head of mission to one or more other States it may establish a diplomatic mission headed by a chargé d'affaires ad interim in each State where the head of mission has not his permanent seat.

3. A head of mission or any member of the diplomatic staff of the mission may act as representative of the sending State to any international organization.

## Article 6

Two or more States may accredit the same person as head of mission to another State, unless objection is offered by the receiving State.

## Article 7

Subject to the provisions of articles 5, 8, 9 and 11, the sending State may freely appoint the members of the staff of the mission. In the case of military, naval or air attachés, the receiving State may require their names to be submitted beforehand, for its approval.

## Article 8

1. Members of the diplomatic staff of the mission should in principle be of the nationality of the sending State.
2. Members of the diplomatic staff of the mission may not be appointed from among persons having the nationality of the receiving State, except with the consent of that State which may be withdrawn at any time.

3. The receiving State may reserve the same right with regard to nationals of a third State who are not also nationals of the sending State.

## Article 9

1. The receiving State may at any time and without having to explain its decision, notify the sending State that the head of the mission or any member of the diplomatic staff of the mission is persona non grata or that any other member of the staff of the mission is not acceptable. In any such case, the sending State shall, as appropriate, either recall the person concerned or terminate his functions with the mission. A person may be declared non grata or not acceptable before arriving in the territory of the receiving State.
2. If the sending State refuses or fails within a reasonable period to carry out its obligations under paragraph 1 of this article, the receiving State may refuse to recognize the person concerned as a member of the mission.

## Article 10

1. The Ministry for Foreign Affairs of the receiving State, or such other ministry as may be agreed, shall be notified of:

(a) The appointment of members of the mission, their arrival and their final departure or the termination of their functions with the mission;

(b) The arrival and final departure of a person belonging to the family of a member of the mission and, where appropriate, the fact that a person becomes or ceases to be a member of the family of a member of the mission;

(c) The arrival and final departure of private servants in the employ of persons referred to in subparagraph (a) of this paragraph and, where appropriate, the fact that they are leaving the employ of such persons;

(d) The engagement and discharge of persons resident in the receiving State as members of the mission or private servants entitled to privileges and immunities.

2. Where possible, prior notification of arrival and final departure shall also be given.

## Article 11

1. In the absence of specific agreement as to the size of the mission, the receiving State may require that the size of a mission be kept within limits considered by it to be reasonable and normal, having regard to circumstances and conditions in the receiving State and to the needs of the particular mission.

2. The receiving State may equally, within similar bounds and on a non-discriminatory basis, refuse to accept officials of a particular category.

**Article 12**

The sending State may not, without the prior express consent of the receiving State, establish offices forming part of the mission in localities other than those in which the mission itself is established.

**Article 13**

1. The head of the mission is considered as having taken up his functions in the receiving State either when he has presented his credentials or when he has notified his arrival and a true copy of his credentials has been presented to the Ministry for Foreign Affairs of the receiving State, or such other ministry as may be agreed, in accordance with the practice prevailing in the receiving State which shall be applied in a uniform manner.
2. The order of presentation of credentials or of a true copy thereof will be determined by the date and time of the arrival of the head of the mission.

## Article 14

1. Heads of mission are divided into three classes, namely:
(a) That of ambassadors or nuncios accredited to Heads of State, and other heads of mission of equivalent rank;
(b) That of envoys, ministers and internuncios accredited to Heads of State;
(c) That of chargés d'affaires accredited to Ministers for Foreign Affairs.
2. Except as concerns precedence and etiquette, there shall be no differentiation between heads of mission by reason of their class.

## Article 15

The class to which the heads of their missions are to be assigned shall be agreed between States.

## Article 16

1. Heads of mission shall take precedence in their respective classes in the order of the date and time of taking up their functions in accordance with article 13.
2. Alterations in the credentials of a head of mission not involving any change of class shall not affect his precedence.

3. This article is without prejudice to any practice accepted by the receiving State regarding the precedence of the representative of the Holy See.

## Article 17

The precedence of the members of the diplomatic staff of the mission shall be notified by the head of the mission to the Ministry for Foreign Affairs or such other ministry as may be agreed.

## Article 18

The procedure to be observed in each State for the reception of heads of mission shall be uniform in respect of each class.

## Article 19

1. If the post of head of the mission is vacant, or if the head of the mission is unable to perform his functions a chargé d'affaires ad interim shall act provisionally as head of the mission. The name of the chargé d'affaires ad interim shall be notified, either by the head of the mission or, in case he is unable to do so, by the Ministry for Foreign Affairs of the sending State to the Ministry for Foreign Affairs of the receiving State or such other ministry as may be agreed.

2. In cases where no member of the diplomatic staff of the mission is present in the receiving State, a member of the administrative and technical staff may, with the consent of the receiving State, be designated by the sending State to be in charge of the current administrative affairs of the mission.

## Article 20

The mission and its head shall have the right to use the flag and emblem of the sending State on the premises of the mission, including the residence of the head of the mission, and on his means of transport.

## Article 21

1. The receiving State shall either facilitate the acquisition on its territory, in accordance with its laws, by the sending State of premises necessary for its mission or assist the latter in obtaining accommodation in some other way.
2. It shall also, where necessary, assist missions in obtaining suitable accommodation for their members.

## Article 22

1. The premises of the mission shall be inviolable. The agents of the receiving State may not enter them, except with the consent of the head of the mission.
2. The receiving State is under a special duty to take all appropriate steps to protect the premises of the mission against any intrusion or damage and to prevent any disturbance of the peace of the mission or impairment of its dignity.
3. The premises of the mission, their furnishings and other property thereon and the means of transport of the mission shall be immune from search, requisition, attachment or execution.

## Article 23

1. The sending State and the head of the mission shall be exempt from all national, regional or municipal dues and taxes in respect of the premises of the mission, whether owned or leased, other than such as represent payment for specific services rendered.
2. The exemption from taxation referred to in this article shall not apply to such dues and taxes payable under the law of the receiving State by persons contracting with the sending State or the head of the mission.

## Article 24

The archives and documents of the mission shall be inviolable at any time and wherever they may be.

## Article 25

The receiving State shall accord full facilities for the performance of the functions of the mission.

## Article 26

Subject to its laws and regulations concerning zones entry into which is prohibited or regulated for reasons of national security, the receiving State shall ensure to all members of the mission freedom of movement and travel in its territory.

## Article 27

1. The receiving State shall permit and protect free communication on the part of the mission for all official purposes. In communicating with the Government and the other missions and consulates of the sending State, wherever situated, the mission may employ all appropriate means, including diplomatic couriers and messages in code or cipher.

However, the mission may install and use a wireless transmitter only with the consent of the receiving State.

2. The official correspondence of the mission shall be inviolable. Official correspondence means all correspondence relating to the mission and its functions.
3. The diplomatic bag shall not be opened or detained.
4. The packages constituting the diplomatic bag must bear visible external marks of their character and may contain only diplomatic documents or articles intended for official use.
5. The diplomatic courier, who shall be provided with an official document indicating his status and the number of packages constituting the diplomatic bag, shall be protected by the receiving State in the performance of his functions. He shall enjoy person inviolability and shall not be liable to any form of arrest or detention.
6. The sending State or the mission may designate diplomatic couriers ad hoc. In such cases the provisions of paragraph 5 of this article shall also apply, except that the immunities therein mentioned shall cease to apply when such a courier has delivered to the consignee the diplomatic bag in his charge.
7. A diplomatic bag may be entrusted to the captain of a commercial aircraft scheduled to land at an authorized port of entry. He shall be provided with an official document indicating the number of packages constituting the bag but he shall not be considered to be a diplomatic courier. The mission may send

one of its members to take possession of the diplomatic bag directly and freely from the captain of the aircraft.

## Article 28

The fees and charges levied by the mission in the course of its official duties shall be exempt from
all dues and taxes.

## Article 29

The person of a diplomatic agent shall be inviolable. He shall not be liable to any form of arrest or detention. The receiving State shall treat him with due respect and shall take all appropriate steps to prevent any attack on his person, freedom or dignity.

## Article 30

1. The private residence of a diplomatic agent shall enjoy the same inviolability and protection as the premises of the mission.
2. His papers, correspondence and, except as provided in paragraph 3 of article 31, his property, shall likewise enjoy inviolability.

## Article 31

1. A diplomatic agent shall enjoy immunity from the criminal jurisdiction of the receiving State. He shall also enjoy immunity from its civil and administrative jurisdiction, except in the case of:
(a) A real action relating to private immovable property situated in the territory of the receiving State, unless he holds it on behalf of the sending State for the purposes of the mission;
(b) An action relating to succession in which the diplomatic agent is involved as executor, administrator, heir or legatee as a private person and not on behalf of the sending State;
(c) An action relating to any professional or commercial activity exercised by the diplomatic agent in the receiving State outside his official functions.
2. A diplomatic agent is not obliged to give evidence as a witness.
3. No measures of execution may be taken in respect of a diplomatic agent except in the cases coming under subparagraphs (a), (b) and (c) of paragraph 1 of this article, and provided that the measures concerned can be taken without infringing the inviolability of his person or of his residence.
4. The immunity of a diplomatic agent from the jurisdiction of the receiving State does not exempt him from the jurisdiction of the sending State.

## Article 32

1. The immunity from jurisdiction of diplomatic agents and of persons enjoying immunity under article 37 may be waived by the sending State.
2. Waiver must always be express.
3. The initiation of proceedings by a diplomatic agent or by a person enjoying immunity from jurisdiction under article 37 shall preclude him from invoking immunity from jurisdiction in respect of any counterclaim directly connected with the principal claim.
4. Waiver of immunity from jurisdiction in respect of civil or administrative proceedings shall not be held to imply waiver of immunity in respect of the execution of the judgement, for which a separate waiver shall be necessary.

## Article 33

1. Subject to the provisions of paragraph 3 of this article, a diplomatic agent shall with respect to services rendered for the sending State be exempt from social security provisions which may be in force in the receiving State.
2. The exemption provided for in paragraph 1 of this article shall also apply to private servants who are in the sole employ of a diplomatic agent, on condition:

(a) That they are not nationals of or permanently resident in the receiving State; and

(b) That they are covered by the social security provisions which may be in force in the sending State or a third State.

3. A diplomatic agent who employs persons to whom the exemption provided for in paragraph 2 of this article does not apply shall observe the obligations which the social security provisions of the receiving State impose upon employers.

4. The exemption provided for in paragraphs 1 and 2 of this article shall not preclude voluntary participation in the social security system of the receiving State provided that such participation is permitted by that State.

5. The provisions of this article shall not affect bilateral or multilateral agreements concerning social security concluded previously and shall not prevent the conclusion of such agreements in the future.

## Article 34

A diplomatic agent shall be exempt from all dues and taxes, personal or real, national, regional or municipal, except:

(a) Indirect taxes of a kind which are normally incorporated in the price of goods or services;

(b) Dues and taxes on private immovable property situated in the territory of the receiving State, unless he holds it on behalf of the sending State for the purposes of the mission;

(c) Estate, succession or inheritance duties levied by the receiving State, subject to the provisions of paragraph 4 of article 39;

(d) Dues and taxes on private income having its source in the receiving State and capital taxes on investments made in commercial undertakings in the receiving State;

(e) Charges levied for specific services rendered;

(f) Registration, court or record fees, mortgage dues and stamp duty, with respect to immovable property, subject to the provisions of article 23.

## Article 35

The receiving State shall exempt diplomatic agents from all personal services, from all public service of any kind whatsoever, and from military obligations such as those connected with requisitioning, military contributions and billeting.

## Article 36

1. The receiving State shall, in accordance with such laws and regulations as it may adopt, permit entry of and grant exemption from all customs duties, taxes, and related charges

other than charges for storage, cartage and similar services, on:

(a) Articles for the official use of the mission;
(b) Articles for the personal use of a diplomatic agent or members of his family forming part of his household, including articles intended for his establishment.

2. The personal baggage of a diplomatic agent shall be exempt from inspection, unless there are serious grounds for presuming that it contains articles not covered by the exemptions mentioned in paragraph 1 of this article, or articles the import or export of which is prohibited by the law or controlled by the quarantine regulations of the receiving State. Such inspection shall be conducted only in the presence of the diplomatic agent or of his authorized representative.

## Article 37

1. The members of the family of a diplomatic agent forming part of his household shall, if they are not nationals of the receiving State, enjoy the privileges and immunities specified in articles 29 to 36.
2. Members of the administrative and technical staff of the mission, together with members of their families forming part of their respective households, shall, if they are not nationals of or permanently resident in the receiving State, enjoy the

privileges and immunities specified in articles 29 to 35, except that the immunity from civil and administrative jurisdiction of the receiving State specified in paragraph 1 of article 31 shall not extend to acts performed outside the course of their duties. They shall also enjoy the privileges specified in article 36, paragraph 1, in respect of articles imported at the time of first installation.

3. Members of the service staff of the mission who are not nationals of or permanently resident in the receiving State shall enjoy immunity in respect of acts performed in the course of their duties, exemption from dues and taxes on the emoluments they receive by reason of their employment and the exemption contained in article 33.

4. Private servants of members of the mission shall, if they are not nationals of or permanently resident in the receiving State, be exempt from dues and taxes on the emoluments they receive by reason of their employment. In other respects, they may enjoy privileges and immunities only to the extent admitted by the receiving State. However, the receiving State must exercise its jurisdiction over those persons in such a manner as not to interfere unduly with the performance of the functions of the mission.

## Article 38

1. Except insofar as additional privileges and immunities may be granted by the receiving State, a diplomatic agent who is a national of or permanently resident in that State shall enjoy only immunity from jurisdiction, and inviolability, in respect of official acts performed in the exercise of his functions.
2. Other members of the staff of the mission and private servants who are nationals of or permanently resident in the receiving State shall enjoy privileges and immunities only to the extent admitted by the receiving State. However, the receiving State must exercise its jurisdiction over those persons in such a manner as not to interfere unduly with the performance of the functions of the mission.

## Article 39

1. Every person entitled to privileges and immunities shall enjoy them from the moment he enters the territory of the receiving State on proceeding to take up his post or, if already in its territory, from the moment when his appointment is notified to the Ministry for Foreign Affairs or such other ministry as may be agreed.
2. When the functions of a person enjoying privileges and immunities have come to an end, such privileges and

immunities shall normally cease at the moment when he leaves the country, or on expiry of a reasonable period in which to do so, but shall subsist until that time, even in case of armed conflict. However, with respect to acts performed by such a person in the exercise of his functions as a member of the mission, immunity shall continue to subsist.

3. In case of the death of a member of the mission, the members of his family shall continue to enjoy the privileges and immunities to which they are entitled until the expiry of a reasonable period in which to leave the country.

4. In the event of the death of a member of the mission not a national of or permanently resident in the receiving State or a member of his family forming part of his household, the receiving State shall permit the withdrawal of the movable property of the deceased, with the exception of any property acquired in the country the export of which was prohibited at the time of his death. Estate, succession and inheritance duties shall not be levied on movable property the presence of which in the receiving State was due solely to the presence there of the deceased as a member of the mission or as a member of the family of a member of the mission.

# Article 40

1. If a diplomatic agent passes through or is in the territory of a third State, which has granted him a passport visa if such visa was necessary, while proceeding to take up or to return to his post, or when returning to his own country, the third State shall accord him inviolability and such other immunities as may be required to ensure his transit or return. The same shall apply in the case of any members of his family enjoying privileges or immunities who are accompanying the diplomatic agent, or travelling separately to join him or to return to their country.
2. In circumstances similar to those specified in paragraph 1 of this article, third States shall not hinder the passage of members of the administrative and technical or service staff of a mission, and of members of their families, through their territories.
3. Third States shall accord to official correspondence and other official communications in transit, including messages in code or cipher, the same freedom and protection as is accorded by the receiving State. They shall accord to diplomatic couriers, who have been granted a passport visa if such visa was necessary, and diplomatic bags in transit, the same inviolability and protection as the receiving State is bound to accord.
4. The obligations of third States under paragraphs 1, 2 and 3 of this article shall also apply to the persons mentioned

respectively in those paragraphs, and to official communications and diplomatic bags, whose presence in the territory of the third State is due to force majeure.

## Article 41

1. Without prejudice to their privileges and immunities, it is the duty of all persons enjoying such privileges and immunities to respect the laws and regulations of the receiving State. They also have a duty not to interfere in the internal affairs of that State.
2. All official business with the receiving State entrusted to the mission by the sending State shall be conducted with or through the Ministry for Foreign Affairs of the receiving State or such other ministry as may be agreed.
3. The premises of the mission must not be used in any manner incompatible with the functions of the mission as laid down in the present Convention or by other rules of general international law or by any special agreements in force between the sending and the receiving State.

## Article 42

A diplomatic agent shall not in the receiving State practise for personal profit any professional or commercial activity.

## Article 43

The function of a diplomatic agent comes to an end, inter alia:
(a) On notification by the sending State to the receiving State that the function of the diplomatic agent has come to an end;
(b) On notification by the receiving State to the sending State that, in accordance with paragraph 2 of article 9, it refuses to recognize the diplomatic agent as a member of the mission.

## Article 44

The receiving State must, even in case of armed conflict, grant facilities in order to enable persons enjoying privileges and immunities, other than nationals of the receiving State, and members of the families of such persons irrespective of their nationality, to leave at the earliest possible moment. It must, in particular, in case of need, place at their disposal the necessary means of transport for themselves and their property.

## Article 45

If diplomatic relations are broken off between two States, or if a mission is permanently or temporarily recalled:

(a) The receiving State must, even in case of armed conflict, respect and protect the premises of the mission, together with its property and archives;

(b) The sending State may entrust the custody of the premises of the mission, together with its property and archives, to a third State acceptable to the receiving State;

(c) The sending State may entrust the protection of its interests and those of its nationals to a third State acceptable to the receiving State.

## Article 46

A sending State may with the prior consent of a receiving State, and at the request of a third State not represented in the receiving State, undertake the temporary protection of the interests of the third State and of its nationals.

## Article 47

1. In the application of the provisions of the present Convention, the receiving State shall not discriminate as between States.
2. However, discrimination shall not be regarded as taking place:

(a) Where the receiving State applies any of the provisions of the present Convention restrictively because of a restrictive application of that provision to its mission in the sending State;

(b) Where by custom or agreement States extend to each other more favourable treatment than is required by the provisions of the present Convention.

## Article 48

The present Convention shall be open for signature by all States Members of the United Nations or of any of the specialized agencies Parties to the Statute of the International Court of Justice, and by any other State invited by the General Assembly of the United Nations to become a Party to the Convention, as follows: until 31 October 1961 at the Federal Ministry for Foreign Affairs of Austria and subsequently, until 31 March 1962, at the United Nations Headquarters in New York.

## Article 49

The present Convention is subject to ratification. The instruments of ratification shall be deposited with the Secretary-General of the United Nations.

## Article 50

The present Convention shall remain open for accession by any State belonging to any of the four categories mentioned in article 48. The instruments of accession shall be deposited with the SecretaryGeneral of the United Nations.

## Article 51

1. The present Convention shall enter into force on the thirtieth day following the date of deposit of the twenty-second instrument of ratification or accession with the Secretary-General of the Unitet Nations.
2. For each State ratifying or acceding to the Convention after the deposit of the twenty-second instrument of ratification or accession, the Convention shall enter into force on the thirtieth day after deposit by such State of its instrument of ratification or accession.

## Article 52

The Secretary-General of the United Nations shall inform all States belonging to any of the four categories mentioned in article 48:

(a) Of signatures to the present Convention and of the deposit of instruments of ratification or accession, in accordance with articles 48, 49 and 50;

(b) Of the date on which the present Convention will enter into force, in accordance with article 51.

## Article 53

The original of the present Convention, of which the Chinese, English, French, Russian and Spanish texts are equally authentic, shall be deposited with the Secretary-General of the United Nations, who shall send certified copies thereof to all States belonging to any of the four categories mentioned in article 48.

IN WITNESS WHEREOF the undersigned Plenipotentiaries, being duly authorized thereto by their respective Governments, have signed the present Convention.

DONE at Vienna this eighteenth day of April one thousand nine hundred and sixty-one